Unveiling the Hidden Words

I dedicate this book to the memory of
SHOGHI EFFENDI
for his matchless translations of Bahá'u'lláh's utterances

and

With gratitude to my parents,
EDWARD AND VIOLA GRAU,
without whose unstinting support this book
would not have become a reality

Unveiling the Hidden Words

The Norms Used by Shoghi Effendi
In His Translation of the Hidden Words

by

Diana Lorice Malouf

George Ronald
Oxford

GEORGE RONALD, Publisher
46 High Street, Kidlington, Oxford OX5 2DN

British Library Cataloguing in Publication Data

*A catalogue record for this book is available
from the British Library*

ISBN 0-85398-414-X pbk

Printed and bound by The Cromwell Press, Melksham, Wiltshire

Contents

Acknowledgements

I would like to thank the many people who have encouraged and assisted me over the years I have been working on this project. I extend genuine appreciation to my dissertation committee for their efforts on my behalf. In particular, I am grateful to my committee supervisor, Dr Marilyn Gaddis Rose, for her painstaking work in repeatedly editing the manuscript and for the advice and guidance given me during the years I was in Binghamton at the State University of New York. Also I am indebted to Dr Norman Stillman for his helpful suggestions and several rereadings which he generously continued to offer during his sabbatical. Dr Frederick Garber also read the dissertation during his sabbatical, and Dr Donald Peretz, outside reader, consented to evaluate my work on very short notice.

I thank the Bahá'ís of Broome County for their love and assistance and, in indirect ways, sharing in this undertaking, especially Kay P. Dailey and Joe Noyes (both now deceased), Dorothy Holmlund and Dr Valerie Perdue. I shall always be grateful.

To my brother, Robert Malouf, and especially, my parents, Edward and Viola Grau, who lent me their aid and support, words are inadequate to convey my sentiments. And to my son, Hassan Malouf, I give loving thanks for his sacrifice of those hours I gave both to dissertation and book which might have gone to him.

I extend gratitude to those who believed in the contribution of my research in translation studies and The Hidden Words to future scholarship and looked forward to its conversion into book form, in particular Dr Robert Stockman and Dr Peter Khan.

I wish to thank and commend my editor at George Ronald, Publisher, Wendi Momen, who through her very capable and tireless efforts and efficient and expeditious editing of the manuscript prepared it for publication. I owe her a debt of thanks.

Diana Lorice Malouf

1

Introduction

Translation Studies as a distinct discipline is a recent effort to answer the ancient problem of literary man: the transposition of one linguistic system into another – perhaps from the same language family or from a remote one; from a similar cultural environment with its accompanying historic, social and artistic ties, or from one far removed; from a close literary tradition or a vastly different one. The problem has long been with us, as evinced in the story of the Tower of Babel. And the present-day translator may often feel that no matter how noble and conscientious his attempts to translate a literary text, he is, indeed, thrown into as much confusion as his legendary literary forebears.

In no area of translation endeavours does the challenge seem more acute than that of translating writings that are considered to be nothing less than the Word of God – the holy scriptures of the world's major religions, revealed in their original tongues – into other world languages. Yet the world's religious texts are translated into far more languages and dialects than other texts, fiction or otherwise. No field of literary translation compounds the challenges, evokes more bitter cries of frustration and woe or poses more problems than translating scripture. The responsibility of the translator weighs more heavily when dealing with sacred texts and censure looms more reprehensible when, in addition to couching the text in language suitable to its station, the translator must also maintain the closest fidelity possible to the meaning of the original. What may be relatively unimportant in other translation here becomes burdensome.

Little wonder, then, that the Bible, for instance, has been translated by one group then retranslated by another, each seeking to emphasize some aspect or other: beauty in the King James translation, current-day vernacular in the more recent versions, and so forth.

Meaning assumes paramount importance in the translation of scripture. Yet the translator must interpret as fact the text he is recreating in the target language and is, of course, in his function of interpretation, subject to his own limitations, impressions, biases and doctrinal affiliations. In other words, we each perceive the world differently; no two of us are alike and neither are any two translations by different translators of the same text. If ten translators, for example, are given the same text to work on independently, they will come up with ten distinct translations, with subtle or overt differences. Traditionally, no other area of translation has evoked more nit-picking and hair-splitting arguments over the true meaning of a word and its translation than has the Word of God. In religious history no one has been both translator and authorized interpreter of a major religion's scripture.

Thus Shoghi Effendi is unique. Not only was he both Guardian of the Bahá'í Faith and its Expounder, or authorized and infallible interpreter, he also translated many of the major Bahá'í scriptures from their original languages into English. The world's great religions, revealed through the ages – Judaism, Christianity, Islam, Zoroastrianism, Buddhism and Hinduism – did not provide an uncontested successor to their founders. While allusions to such successors have been made by the founders of those religions – for example, Christ said, 'Thou art Peter and upon this rock I will build my church' – such unwritten statements have long been disputed as to meaning and have even been fought over. Bahá'u'lláh, however, in an undisputable Covenant, named His son 'Abdu'l-Bahá as Interpreter and Head of the Bahá'í community after His death; and 'Abdu'l-Bahá, in turn, in a written Will and Testament, named Shoghi Effendi as

Guardian of the Bahá'í Faith and the divinely authorized Expounder of its teachings after 'Abdu'l-Bahá's passing.

Although Shoghi Effendi's translations of scripture include three book-length works, one of which is the Hidden Words; two book-length compilations; various letters (known as Tablets); a booklet of prayers; and numerous excerpts from the writings of the three central figures of the Bahá'í Faith, which he quotes generously in his many English works and correspondence, he translated only a very small percentage of the Bahá'í sacred writings, which are the works of the Báb, Bahá'u'lláh and 'Abdu'l-Bahá. However, those works he did translate remain in a class by themselves since they are not only translations but also interpretations.

At this point we are tempted to look back in history to compare other translators with Shoghi Effendi and to determine whether his position as authorized interpreter is, in fact, unique. St Jerome quickly comes to mind. He was commissioned by Pope Damasus I to edit a standard Latin version of the Bible which he worked on for 30 years. It was completed around 404 AD and his Vulgate was the official Bible of the Church for over a thousand years. However, even with the endorsement of Augustine and other church leaders, it did not immediately win acceptance, and during copying, parts of the older Latin version were interpolated into it. Scholars tried to remove these interpolations during the Middle Ages but when printing made a standard edition necessary there was none available. The Vulgate also appeared in new editions such as the Clementine Vulgate, named after Pope Clement VIII, in 1590 and revised in 1592, and the new edition commissioned in 1907 by Pope Pius X, the first volume of which appeared in 1926.

Obviously in St Jerome's case there was no written documentation by the founder of Christianity or even from the Church according him the position of divinely authorized interpreter or translator. In addition, older translations still circulated and even found their way via copyists into Jerome's Vulgate. Although his Vulgate endured as the official Bible for over a thousand years, greatly affected Western culture and language, and is one of the world's most notable translations, St Jerome was not an authorized, infallible interpreter of the Bible he so ably rendered into Latin.

Let us now turn to Martin Luther, whose prodigious translation of the Bible into German – the New Testament in 1522 and the complete Bible in 1534 – is still the favoured translation among German Protestants to this day. His translation greatly affected the development of the German tongue and was used as a basis of translation into other languages.

Again, however, though Luther is the acknowledged founder of the Reformation, nowhere is there written authorization for him to interpret scripture; neither did he postulate himself as an infallible interpreter or translator. He did, of course, reinterpret certain notions of Christianity which became the hallmarks of Protestant Christendom, but he never claimed that his translation was divinely authorized.

The closest precedent to Shoghi Effendi is the successorship in Islam, disputed to this very day, which brought about the major schism of the religion into Sunnism and Shí'ism. It is said that at the Pool of Khumm, the Prophet Muḥammad verbally announced that 'Alí, His son-in-law and the first to believe in Him, was to be His successor. Further, it is related that at His deathbed Muḥammad asked for pen and paper to write down the name of who was to succeed Him; however, His wish was not granted. Immediately upon His death.His followers became divided. A Caliph was chosen by vote, following tribal custom, and Abu-Bakr became the first Caliph of Islam. The Sunnís accepted this succession and did not attribute any divinely authorized function of interpretation to the Caliphs.

For the Shí'ís, though, who followed 'Alí, divinely authorized interpretation of the Qur'án existed for a period of two hundred years, spanning the lives of the twelve Imáms who were the lineal descendants of 'Alí. Their writings have greatly enriched the understanding of the Qur'án.

There are distinctions, obviously, between the successor-ship of the twelve Imáms and that of Shoghi Effendi. For example, the Imáms' right to speak and act as authorized interpreters of the Qur'án was not given to them in written form by Muḥammad, while their position was, and still is, disputed by the majority of the followers of Islam. Had there been a document in the hand of the Prophet, schism could have been prevented, a schism that has cost the lives of countless believers down through the ages. Furthermore, it should be noted that the Imams did not translate their commentaries or treatises.[1]

As to translators within a secular 'religion', Communism, we may call to mind Frederick Engels's editing of the first volume of *Das Kapital*, translated by Samuel Moore and Edward Aveling. Though Engels carefully oversaw the trans-lation of this major work which his friend of 40 years pub-lished in 1867, some recent translations are looked upon as superior to the translation Engels edited. Some of Marx's works which were in the possession of the German Social Democrats were purchased by the Soviet Union and kept at the Marxist–Leninist Institute in Moscow. Here the works were interpreted by Soviet scholars but the originals were not released. When these documents were finally made available, new translations, apparently influenced by some of these works, were made possible.

Thus even in the secular 'religion' of Communism, in which Engels's works are considered authorized core litera-ture (and accepting that editing a translation is equivalent to translating it) Engels's editing of the translation of the third edition has not remained standard and scholars now turn as first choice to newer translations. Of course, we may look at Engels as the interpreter and elaborator of Marx's work, although such a position is by association and not by, for example, Marx's written statement that Engels should act in this capacity.

Thus in Shoghi Effendi's appointment as authorized interpreter we have an instance unique in religious history.

His translation of the sacred writings of Bahá'u'lláh – from the Bahá'í perspective – cannot be disputed as to meaning and import. His authorized translations are a first. In the following pages we shall examine the translation norms he utilized in his translation of the Hidden Words of Bahá'u'lláh in the light of this authority.

The study of norms is important to an understanding of the translation process. The concept of norms in translation has its corollary in societal norms. Toury defines the relationship thus:

> Literary Translation, like any other behavioural activity, is subject to constraints of several types and varying degree. These constraints can be described along a scale anchored between two extremes; objective, relatively absolute rules (in certain behavioural domains, even stable, formulated laws) on the one hand, and fully subjective idiosyncrasies on the other. In between these two poles lies a middle-ground occupied in intersubjective factors, commonly designated 'norms'. The norms themselves do not occupy merely one point of the scale, but a graduated section of the entire continuum.
>
> Sociologists and social psychologists regard norms as the translation of general values or ideas shared by a certain community – as to what is right and wrong, adequate and inadequate – into specific performance-instructions appropriate for and applicable to specific situations, providing they are not yet formulated as laws.[2]

Although norms are not laws, they do act as a form of control and order – in literature as well as in other facets of life. In literature they allow a literary system to exist, for without them there would be no regularity in, predictability or cohesion of the literary system and, hence, no guide for the writer either to adhere to or break, within limits, thereby stimulating the evolution of a part of that system. Beyond norms there is the behaviour of the translator. This is not norm-governed and can only be explained in terms of idiosyncrasy, or subjective behaviour, which occurs with all translators at one time or another but does not govern the majority of choices, which are usually norm-governed.

The investigation of the norms Shoghi Effendi used in his translation of the Hidden Words will throw light on his function of interpreter and will, it is hoped, broaden our assessment of how norms act in a translation. This operation of norms, how they work and how they are utilized is highlighted for two reasons: 1) the translation is especially important because it is scripture and, therefore, traditionally carries more weight and importance than other literary texts; and 2) it is not simply translation but translation made, from a Bahá'í point of view, by a divinely authorized Expounder. These two important distinctions should bring into clearer focus the function and utilization of norms and, it is hoped, will add to the possibility of helping to build a viable theory of translation or, at least, providing a firmer grasp on its workings.

2

Shoghi Effendi

Education

Shoghi Effendi (1897–1957), the great grandson of Bahá'u-'lláh (1817-92), founder of the Bahá'í Faith and author of the Hidden Words, was born in the prison-city of Acre, Palestine. Bahá'u'lláh and His family had been exiled from Iran in 1853. Bahá'u'lláh spent ten years in Baghdad, was sent to Constantinople for four months and to Adrianople for five years, and finally arrived in Acre on 31 August 1868, where He died in 1892 after 40 years of imprisonment. Shoghi Effendi was born in the house of his grandfather, 'Abdu'l-Bahá, the son of Bahá'u'lláh. 'Abdu'l-Bahá was designated by Bahá'u'lláh as the head of the Bahá'í Faith after Bahá'u'lláh's death. Shoghi Effendi's mother was the eldest of 'Abdu'l-Bahá's four daughters and he was the first grandchild. Shoghi Effendi's earliest education took place in 'Abdu'l-Bahá's home, which also housed the extended family. 'Abdu'l-Bahá held a great and special love for this grandson. He named him 'Shoghi', which means 'longing, yearning', and always addressed him by the title 'Effendi', which means 'sir' or 'mister'. 'Abdu'l-Bahá insisted that the family also use this title for him. Shoghi Effendi used this title as his name from the time he became Guardian in 1921 and all his literary works are penned under it.

Shoghi Effendi's earliest education, in accordance with 'Abdu'l-Bahá's writings on the subject of the education of children, was in manners and morals. Manners and courtesy were primary requisites in the household of 'Abdu'l-Bahá

9

and were highly prized attributes.[3] We have evidence that Shoghi Effendi developed a moral sense in his very early years. For example, the only time he would offend his play-mates was when they were 'cheating or plotting' and even then he would make up with them before retiring for the night.[4] Piety and devotion were virtues he developed in his earliest childhood.

'Abdu'l-Bahá's first Tablet to Shoghi Effendi (the term 'Tablet' designates a written communication) was in response to five-year-old Shoghi Effendi's request that his grandfather write something for him:

> He is God!
> O My Shoghi, I have no time to talk, leave me alone! You said 'write' – I have written. What else should be done? Now is not the time for you to read and write, it is the time for jumping about and chanting 'O my God!', therefore memo-rize the prayers of the Blessed Beauty and chant them that I may hear them, because there is no time for anything else.[5]

According to the translator of the Tablet, Dr Baghdadi, a physician who was an intimate of the family, Shoghi Effendi sent 'letters' to 'Abdu'l-Bahá:

> Shoghi Effendi's first Tablet was an answer to some of his letters that he had written in my room. I have seen these letters and even in one of them he had two poetic verses in Arabic which I had composed in praise of 'Abdu'l-Bahá. Shoghi Effendi, though only five years of age, wanted to know why he would not be given the chance at that age to learn higher sciences and arts, etc.[6]

Several questions about these 'letters' to 'Abdu'l-Bahá arise but owing to lack of evidence we can only guess their an-swers: Were these real letters or merely childish scribbling? Did the small boy actually write them in his own hand or did he dictate them to Dr Baghdadi, who wrote them down?

What language(s) were they in? Even without the answers there are revealing factors in this passage. For a child to want to learn 'higher sciences and arts' is surely a sign of precocity, as is the awareness that the formal Persian epistolary style demands the inclusion of lines of poetry. We also see an early interest in matters literary and a glimmer in the boy of the genius of the man. Dr Baghdadi goes on to write:

> On receiving and learning the contents of this Tablet, Shoghi Effendi at once memorized a number of Bahá'u'lláh's prayers and began to chant them so loudly that the whole neighbourhood could hear his voice. His parents and other members of the Holy Family asked him to lower his voice. 'The Master wrote to me to chant that He may hear me. I am doing my best.' And he kept chanting at the top of his voice for many hours each day.[7]

This passage is of particular interest in that it indicates at what an early age Shoghi Effendi began to apply himself to chanting, which is a musical art form in the Middle East and one to which expert chanters devote a lifetime of study and application. It is my contention that Shoghi Effendi's development of this musical form, which is so tied into language, is the key to the very high degree of musicality found in his English translation of the Hidden Words. This is examined in greater depth in chapter 6. Suffice it for now to explore the type, manner and progression of this aspect of his education so that we may lay the groundwork for a later discussion of its literary application.

Learning to chant was an important aspect of Shoghi Effendi's training. In the Islamic East there is a long tradition of the chanting of prayers in a melodious voice, the recitation or chanting of the verses of the Qur'án, the Muslim holy book, being its highest expression. There is no doubt that in 'Abdu'l-Bahá's household, where Shoghi Effendi grew up, chanting was highly regarded:

The childhood nurse of Shoghi Effendi used to recount that when he was still a baby the Master was wont to call one of the Muslims who chanted in the mosque to come at least once a week and chant to the child, in his melodious voice, the sublime verses of the Qur'án. The Master Himself, the Guardian's mother and many others in the household had fine voices. All of this must have deeply affected Shoghi Effendi, who continued to chant to the end of his life. He had an indescribable, full voice, neither very high nor very low, clear, with a beautiful cadence in speaking, whether in English or Persian, and even more beautiful when he chanted in Arabic or Persian.[8]

One who is accomplished in chanting has succeeded in a complicated and rigorous discipline. Apparently 'Abdu'l-Bahá chose a qualified, professional person to teach this art in the household, and one may assume that given Shoghi Effendi's quick mind and facility for chanting, as attested here and by other sources, the effects of this initial tutoring were deeply planted. Memorization is a basic teaching tool of Quranic schools. It may be that the chanter taught at a Quranic school at the mosque and employed this form of education, respected throughout the Middle East. It is probable that he taught the children of 'Abdu'l-Bahá's household and other members of the family to chant passages they knew and to refine them once completely memorized. Shoghi Effendi was the first to memorize and chant 'Abdu'l-Bahá's prayer for children:

> . . . he had memorized some touching passages written by 'Abdu'l-Bahá after the ascension of Bahá'u'lláh and when he chanted these the tears would roll down the earnest little face. From another source we are told that when the Master was requested by a western friend, at that time living in His home, to reveal a prayer for children He did so, and the first to memorize it and chant it was Shoghi Effendi who would also chant it in the meetings of the friends.[9]

12

Two observations about Shoghi Effendi arise from this passage. The first is his unusual gift for feeling musical expression and his sensitivity for words of eloquence and pathos. It is not perhaps unusual for an adult to be moved to tears from the musical expression of the written word but it is surprising to find such a response coming from a small child who generally would not yet have developed the musical and literary sensibilities to respond so emotionally. Great music and great literature can, indeed, and, in fact, should, elicit a strong emotional response. Here, it seems, we have indication of a special sensibility to music and to the poetic prose with which 'Abdu'l-Bahá composed these and other prayers. The second thing to note is that Shoghi Effendi chanted the prayer for children 'in the meetings of the friends'. We can say, then, that he did this on several occasions. Either all the children of the household, including Shoghi Effendi, were encouraged to chant at gatherings of the believers, or Shoghi Effendi was exceptional in the quality of his chanting and was, therefore, asked to chant at gatherings. If the second is the case – and this seems most likely – then he not only had pathos and emotion in his chanting but was musically gifted. We might liken this to a small child in our society playing a musical instrument and giving a demonstration for family and friends. The exceptional rhythm and music of the prose Shoghi Effendi uses in the translation of the Hidden Words is, I suggest, a reflection of his finely tuned musical ability expressed in chanting. To the specific application of this sense of musicality we shall return in chapter 6.

Shoghi Effendi's devotion to his grandfather was very great. In turn, 'Abdu'l-Bahá was Shoghi Effendi's primary mentor, not in the sense that He devoted Himself to the exclusive education of the child but in the fact that Shoghi Effendi emulated his grandfather and followed Him about almost as a shadow, such that the exceedingly bright and receptive child must have absorbed, by osmosis, as it were, much knowledge from Him. In this passage written by

Shoghi Effendi's widow, we find 'Abdu'l-Bahá, having returned from His Western journeys in 1913, instructing Shoghi Effendi when he was a youth in the art of chanting:

> . . . the old custom of prayers in the presence of 'Abdu'l-Bahá was resumed and Shoghi Effendi would chant too, with his lovely young voice, and 'Abdu'l-Bahá would sometimes correct and instruct him. There was nothing unusual in this; I myself often heard older members of the family correct the tune or the pronunciation of someone who was reciting verses or poems out loud; no doubt the Master must have done this many times over the years to Shoghi Effendi.[10]

Around the same time 'a Bahá'í going to 'Abdu'l-Bahá's house, early one morning, heard Shoghi Effendi chanting a prayer and 'Abdu'l-Bahá instructing him'.[11] These passages not only indicate with what care Shoghi Effendi was schooled in the nuances of chanting but particularly show us in two documented instances how closely 'Abdu'l-Bahá worked with him in at least this aspect of his education. I would advance that 'Abdu'l-Bahá tutored him in other areas as well. Thus we can say that 'Abdu'l-Bahá was the primary mentor and influence in Shoghi Effendi's life.

In 1902 while 'Abdu'l-Bahá was confined by the Sultan to the prison-city of Acre, Lua Getsinger, an American Bahá'í, came to the city and stayed a year teaching English to 'Abdu'l-Bahá's household.[12] Shoghi Effendi at this time was about six years old. One would assume that Mrs Getsinger held regular, structured classes, something like she herself must have experienced in her own education.

The widow of Shoghi Effendi, Rúḥíyyih Khánum, speaks of two other tutors who taught the grandchildren of 'Abdu'l-Bahá in the household:

> Nevertheless the desire of the child to learn led to the formation of classes in the Master's household for the children, taught by an old Persian believer. I know that at

one time in his childhood, most likely while he was still living in Akka, Shoghi Effendi and other grandchildren were taught by an Italian, who acted as governess or teacher; a grey-haired elderly lady, she came to call shortly after I was married.[13]

'Alí Na<u>kh</u>javání, who lived in the Holy Land during the lifetime of Shoghi Effendi, also mentions the Italian teacher: 'In the Household the Master also had asked a special European tutor to help in teaching foreign languages to His family.'[14]

The 'old Persian believer' was Mírzá Asadu'lláh-i-Qumí,[15] who was to later accompany 'Abdu'l-Bahá as His attendant on His journeys to Egypt, Europe and America. Mírzá Asadu'lláh taught the children of 'Abdu'l-Bahá's household while they were still resident in Acre, which would put Shoghi Effendi's age at something under ten or eleven years. Mírzá Asadu'lláh, it is safe to assume, taught the children how to read and write Persian, as that was the native language of the family and was spoken in the home. It is possible that he also knew English because he corresponded with some of the American Bahá'ís in 1903.[16] Therefore, he could have taught English but there appears to be no evidence to support this suggestion.

As for the Italian governess, I can find no evidence that Shoghi Effendi knew Italian and we can only guess what subject this teacher may have taught. It is possible that she taught English or French.

From another source, the monthly newspaper of the American Bahá'í community, the *Bahá'í News* for April 1937, we learn that:

> Always he lived with his family in the home of 'Abdu'l-Bahá and there was under the training of the Master from his birth. 'Abdu'l-Bahá had private teachers (two French governesses) in his old prison home for the children in His family . . .[17]

15

This raises several questions. Is there a third or fourth tutor of foreign languages whom we have not yet discussed? Or is one of the French governesses in fact the Italian governess who we could then assume taught French to the children? The *Bahá'í News* indicates that this evidence comes from a reliable source: 'These messages were received either directly from Shoghi Effendi or through his Secretary, to individuals, Communities, Summer School Sessions and the National Assembly.'[18] Thus, it is safe to say that Shoghi Effendi was tutored in French by at least one, and perhaps two, French tutors.

By February 1907 some members of 'Abdu'l-Bahá's family had already moved into 'Abdu'l-Bahá's new house in Haifa.[19] According to his wife, Shoghi Effendi moved to Haifa well before his family moved into 'Abdu'l-Bahá's new house:

> 'Abdu'l-Bahá sent Shoghi Effendi to live in Haifa with his nurse, where already some of the believers resided; at what date this occurred I am unaware, but it was while he was still a young child.[20]

In 1907 Shoghi Effendi would have been about eleven years old. So far as we know, the first school he attended outside the home was 'the Collège des Frères conducted by the Jesuits', considered 'the best school in Haifa'. His wife comments on his school career:

> He told me he had been very unhappy there. Indeed, I gathered from him that he never was really happy in either school or university. In spite of his innately joyous nature, his sensitivity and his background – so different from that of others in every way – could not but set him apart and give rise to many a heart-ache; indeed, he was one of those people whose open and innocent hearts, keen minds and affectionate natures seem to combine to bring upon them more shocks and suffering in life than is the lot of most men. Because of his unhappiness in this school 'Abdu'l-Bahá decided to send him to Beirut where he attended another

Catholic school as a boarder, and where he was equally unhappy. Learning of this in Haifa the family sent a trusted Bahá'í woman to rent a home for Shoghi Effendi in Beirut and take care of and wait on him. It was not long before she wrote to his father that he was very unhappy at school, would refuse to go to it sometimes for days, and was getting thin and run down. His father showed this letter to 'Abdu'l-Bahá Who then had arrangements made for Shoghi Effendi to enter the Syrian Protestant College, which had a school as well as a university, later known as the American College in Beirut, and which the Guardian entered when he finished what was then equivalent to the high school.[21]

It appears Shoghi Effendi entered the Catholic Collège des Frères in 1907 or 1908 and the Catholic school in Beirut shortly afterwards. He spent some time with 'Abdu'l-Bahá in Ramleh, Egypt, a suburb of Alexandria, in October 1910 at the beginning of his grandfather's journey to the West. While there he attended the French Brothers' School and appears to have enrolled for the 1910-11 school year,[22] which runs from early October to after the beginning of July, as correspondence places him there the following April.[23] He may also have been in Ramleh the following academic year, 1911-12, according to his friend and fellow classmate at the French Brothers' School, Ali M. Yazdi: 'The first thing of importance that happened during his stay in Ramleh proved to be a shattering experience.'[24] This was the discovery by Shoghi Effendi that he would not accompany his grandfather on His second Western tour. 'Abdu'l-Bahá sailed for America on 25 March 1912 accompanied by the youthful Shoghi Effendi but Shoghi Effendi was turned back at Naples when he was wrongly diagnosed as having trachoma. Yazdi goes on to say that Shoghi Effendi was depressed and in ill health after his return to Ramleh from this tremendous disappointment.[25] From the context of Yazdi's remarks it would seem that Shoghi Effendi stayed in Ramleh for the rest of the academic year, although he must have been withdrawn from school in anticipation of his trip to America. Thus we can say with some assurance that Shoghi Effendi studied at the French Brothers' School in Ramleh in the 1910-11 and 1911-12 school years. In 1912 'he gives his address from October as that of the Syrian Protestant College in Beirut, Syria, which, he writes, he will be shortly entering'.[26] He matriculated, therefore, in October 1912 for the 1912-13 academic year. 'Abdu'l-Bahá returned to Port Said after His trip to America and Europe on 17 June 1913. On 17 July He travelled to Ramleh. On 1 August Shoghi Effendi came with his family to be with him in Ramleh.[27] According to Yazdi,

> After 'Abdu'l-Bahá's travels in the United States and Europe, He returned to Ramleh for five months. Shoghi Effendi, who had been in Haifa part of that time, came to be with Him. On 2 December 1913 'Abdu'l-Bahá left Alexandria to return to the Holy Land.[28]

Apparently, Shoghi Effendi had returned to Beirut to attend the Protestant Syrian College while his grandfather was abroad. This would have been the school year of 1912-13. However, where Shoghi Effendi was in the autumn of 1913 after going to Ramleh to be with his grandfather is not known. He may have stayed in Ramleh and simply suspended his studies for a term or he may have returned to Beirut to college when the term began in October. The following year he was in Beirut, as a letter dated 3 May 1914 places him at the 'Syrian Protestant College, Beirut, Syria'. In this letter he refers to 'Going back to our college activities our Bahá'í meetings . . .'[29] He graduated on 15 May 1918.[30]

The exact details of Shoghi Effendi's course at the American College at Beirut cannot be ascertained but as facility in English was his primary objective, it is probable that he studied English language and literature. The American University in Beirut was at this time – and up until the 1970s continued to be – the best and most prestigious university in the Middle East and many are the translators that have emerged from its portals. No doubt Shoghi Effendi took advantage of the opportunity to develop and refine his English skills there as had others before him. As it was an American-sponsored university, one would assume that he was exposed to both American and English literary works.

The primary purpose of Shoghi Effendi's education always was to equip him to assist 'Abdu'l-Bahá as His secretary and translator. He fulfilled these roles in the two years he spent in Haifa after taking his Bachelor of Arts degree from the American University in Beirut and before he sailed off to his further studies at Oxford in the spring of 1920. During this time Shoghi Effendi was, for the most part, inseparable from his grandfather, even though his studies were not yet concluded.

As early as 1910 'Abdu'l-Bahá indicated that Shoghi Effendi should study in England. Dr Fallscheer, the German physician of the women of 'Abdu'l-Bahá's household, quoted 'Abdu'l-Bahá in her memoirs:

> At the present time the British Empire is the greatest and is still expanding and its language is a world language. My future Vazir shall receive the preparation for his weighty office in England itself, after he has obtained here in Palestine a fundamental knowledge of the oriental languages and the wisdom of the East.[31]

In the same memoir Dr Fallscheer refers to Oxford as the university which Shoghi Effendi should attend. Eight years later, in the spring of 1920, he did go to England and was enrolled in Balliol College, Oxford University. His purpose in continuing his studies was to translate the Bahá'í writings into English. He planned to resume his work as translator and secretary to 'Abdu'l-Bahá upon his return.[32] Although 'Abdu'l-Bahá was, at this time, in the words of Shoghi Effendi in August 1919, 'indeed in the best of health, physically strong, ever active, revealing hundreds of Tablets a week, perusing innumerable supplications, receiving many visitors and pilgrims',[33] Shoghi Effendi's dream of serving his grandfather was not to be. 'Abdu'l-Bahá passed away on 28 November 1921 while Shoghi Effendi was in England. Shoghi Effendi wrote to a distant cousin in February 1922:

> Ah bitter remorse of having missed Him – in His Last Days – on this earth, I shall take with me to the grave no matter what I may do for Him in future, no matter to what extent my studies in England will repay his wondrous love for me.[34]

These grief-stricken words are further evidence that Shoghi Effendi's studies were directed towards assisting 'Abdu'l-Bahá and indicate that although his grandfather was gone, Shoghi Effendi would still dedicate his life to serving 'Abdu'l-Bahá through his work as Guardian of the Bahá'í Faith.

Perusing Shoghi Effendi's translations of Tablets of 'Abdu'l-Bahá made before his Oxford studies and those done under his term as Guardian, we note a marked difference between them. Although he was fluent in English before studying at Oxford, afterwards we find a master has emerged where once stood the proficient young scholar. Needless to say, being immersed in an English-speaking land and studying at a university of such repute as Oxford refined and polished his translation skills.

Although Shoghi Effendi's goal was a mastery of English that would enable him to translate Bahá'u'lláh's and 'Abdu'l-Bahá's Tablets, it appears that he did not study English language or literature at Oxford. In his wife's biography of him we find the following description of his course of study at Balliol College:

> From a notebook he kept we find the following list, which he had carefully made out, and which shows the dates he began his studies in 1920:
>
> Oct. 14, 1920 Political Science:- Rev. Carlyle
> Oct. 15, 1920 Social and Political Problems:- Mr. Smith
> (Master of Balliol)

Oct. 13, 1920 Social and Industrial Questions:- Rev. Carlyle
Oct. 12, 1920 Political Economy:- Sir T. H. Penson M.A.
Oct. 16, 1920 English Economic History since 1688:- Sir
Penson
Oct. 11, 1920 Logic:- Mr. Ross M.A.
Oct. 12, 1920 Eastern Question:- F. F. Urquhart M.A.
Oct. 19, 1920 Relations of Capital and Labour:- Clay, New
College[35]

The Archivist of Balliol College indicates: 'We have very little information about him . . . I think it likely that he read a "special 'approved course'" for which no syllabus was prescribed. He did not take any degree.'[36] Ali Yazdi, however, indicates that English was one of Shoghi Effendi's subjects at university: 'He was working for a special certificate, not for a Master of Arts or a higher degree. He was studying special subjects – English, economics, history of religion, and so on . . . He was not taking required courses for an advanced degree.'[37] Shoghi Effendi himself stated in a letter to Ali Yazdi,

> My field of study is so *vast*, I have to acquire, master, and digest so many facts, courses, and books – all essential, all indispensable to my future career in the Cause . . . Think of the vast field of Economics; of social conditions and problems; of the various religions of the past, their histories and their principles and their force; the acquisition of a sound and literary ability in English to be served for translation purposes; the mastery of public speaking so essential to me, all these and a dozen more – all to be sought, acquired, and digested![38]

Rúḥíyyih Khánum further explains:

> The Guardian's own idea of why he was at Oxford was quite clear; fortunately we have an expression of this in a letter he wrote to an oriental believer on 18 October 1920: 'My dear spiritual friend . . . God be praised, I am in good health and full of hope and trying to the best of my ability

to equip myself for those things I shall require in my future service to the Cause. My hope is that I may speedily acquire the best that this country and this society have to offer and then return to my home and recast the truths of the Faith in a new form, and thus serve the Holy Threshold.' There is no doubt he was referring to his future translation of the teachings into the perfect English for which he laid the foundation during his sojourn in England.[39]

Shoghi Effendi attended Balliol for one and a half years beginning with the Michaelmas term in the autumn of 1920. He was well into the Michaelmas term of 1921 when he received news of 'Abdu'l-Bahá's death in November and was recalled to Haifa. His work at Balliol left uncompleted, he nevertheless had made great progress during his time at the university. Shortly before his grandfather's passing he wrote to one of the British Bahá'ís, as his wife notes:

> On 22 November 1921, in a letter to one of the English believers, the advances made by Shoghi Effendi in his work at Oxford are clearly reflected; one senses a new mastery and self-assurance: '. . . I have been of late immersed in my work, revising many translations and have sent to Mr Hall my version of Queen Victoria's Tablet.'[40]

The Tablet Shoghi Effendi refers to is one of the Tablets of Bahá'u'lláh addressed to the kings and leaders of the world of His time, here the Queen of England. In this passage Shoghi Effendi indicates that he is translating as well as 'revising many translations', although it is not known whether these were revisions of his own earlier translations or that of other translators. Either way, the translator is at work and will not put down his pen for many years to come.

Language Acquisition

In the previous section we looked at Shoghi Effendi's formal education, which, as we have seen, is intertwined with his acquisition of language. We now turn to a deeper analysis of Shoghi Effendi's language acquisition.

Let us first consider Shoghi Effendi's native language. According to Mr Nakhjavání, who knew Shoghi Effendi well, 'In the Holy Household the language spoken by the family was Persian only.' He goes on to say that the Persian 'servants were also Persian-speaking'.[41]

As noted earlier, Shoghi Effendi began to learn to read and write Persian from Mírzá Asadu'lláh, who tutored him at home. Shoghi Effendi wrote eloquently and masterfully in his native language. 'Doubtless the Master, his parents, the Greatest Holy Leaf [the title of Bahíyyih Khánum, the sister of 'Abdu'l-Bahá], and his teacher, Mírzá Asadu'lláh Qumí' taught him to read and write Persian.[42]

In addition to Persian, Shoghi Effendi also learned Arabic. As previously noted, while Shoghi Effendi was 'still a baby', 'Abdu'l-Bahá asked a Quranic chanter to teach the art of chanting to the household. The Qur'án is written in Arabic, so Shoghi Effendi would have been exposed to Arabic from this experience, although exactly how young he was at the time cannot be ascertained. Furthermore, 'Abdu'l-Bahá, like Bahá'u'lláh before Him, wrote in both Arabic and Persian and the writings of both were often chanted in the house. Throughout Shoghi Effendi's boyhood in the home of his grandfather, morning tea was taken in the presence of 'Abdu'l-Bahá after devotions were chanted in both Arabic and Persian. As Bahá'u'lláh wrote more in Arabic than Persian and 'Abdu'l-Bahá more in Persian than Arabic, both languages would surely have been well-represented at the daily devotions. There is a difference, however, between using a language – particularly Arabic – formally, such as in the chanting of prayers and meditations and being able to converse in it. Indeed, the formal use of written and spoken Arabic is quite different in form from its informal use as a conversational language. Even so, we can piece together a picture of how Shoghi Effendi acquired Arabic.

'Abdu'l-Bahá was 'both fluent and eloquent' in Persian, Arabic and Turkish.[43] As previously noted, 'Abdu'l-Bahá was, it would seem, Shoghi Effendi's primary mentor. No doubt Shoghi Effendi would have tried to emulate his grandfather's verbal and writing skills by learning to speak Arabic. In support of this, 'Alí Nakhjavání notes that 'Shoghi Effendi sometimes accompanied the Master in His visits to homes of the residents in Haifa'.[44] The residents of Haifa were, for the most part, Arabs and spoke Arabic. In addition, a great number of people who sought audience with 'Abdu'l-Bahá were constantly coming into the home and it is likely that many of them also spoke Arabic. Mr Nakhjavání adds that 'he must have spoken to his Arab fellow-students in their language', referring to Shoghi Effendi's move to Haifa, where he attended school. Thus Shoghi Effendi was exposed from the beginning of his life to spoken Arabic and with his inquiring and eager mind would have acquired a knowledge of spoken Arabic as quickly as he could.

'Alí Nakhjavání records that 'Shoghi Effendi learned Arabic as a subject at school . . . He memorized the Writings and prayers, many of which are in Arabic. He also learned Arabic grammar at school.'[45] Although we have no details, it seems logical that in an Arab land one would learn to read and write Arabic from the outset and it is most likely that he studied it at the Jesuit College des Frères in Haifa where he attended school with his 'Arab fellow-students' and where the instruction was in French. He may have studied it when he went to the Catholic school in Beirut, at the French Brothers' School in Ramleh, or at the high school of the Syrian Protestant College. It is unlikely that he postponed such an arduous subject as Arabic until he reached university, as he acquired both an eloquent writing style of his own in Arabic and was able to understand and translate the often difficult writings of Bahá'u'lláh and 'Abdu'l-Bahá in Arabic.

'Abdu'l-Bahá was also fluent in Turkish. 'Everybody under the Ottoman rule had to speak some Turkish to communicate with higher authorities.'[46] In her diary entry for 6

August 1910, Dr Fallscheer, the German woman physician to the women of 'Abdu'l-Bahá's household, records:

> Behia Khanum . . . invited me to take refreshment with her and the ladies of the household . . . we were sipping coffee and talking Turkish, which was easier for me than Arabic . . .[47]

The ladies of the household included Shoghi Effendi's grandmother ('Abdu'l-Bahá's wife, Munírih Khánum), his great-aunt Bahíyyih Khánum, his mother and three aunts ('Abdu'l-Bahá's four daughters) and perhaps others. Since the ladies of the household knew Turkish, it is possible that they taught Shoghi Effendi the language or he might have picked it up from the conversation of the constant stream of visitors who came to see 'Abdu'l-Bahá. As 'Abdu'l-Bahá was Shoghi Effendi's first mentor, the boy probably learned some of the language from Him. It is probable that all three factors contributed to Shoghi Effendi's acquisition of the language. Shoghi Effendi wrote some of his own works in Turkish and was very accomplished in this language.

We now turn to a consideration of the two Western languages Shoghi Effendi knew. According to his wife:

> French was his first foreign language and although in later years he was reluctant to speak it officially, as he felt his fluency in it was rusty through disuse, he retained, at least to my ears, a perfect command of it and invariably did all his addition, like lightning, in French.[48]

Unfortunately, Rúḥíyyih Khánum does not indicate when and where Shoghi Effendi learned French. It is possible he learned it while still a small boy at his grandfather's house in Acre from one of the tutors mentioned earlier. The Italian governess might have taught him French, or, more likely, one of the French governesses gave instruction in French while Shoghi Effendi lived in 'Abdu'l-Bahá's home in Acre.

Shoghi Effendi certainly knew French when he was at school at the Jesuit Collège des Frères in Haifa, which he attended from 1907. The language of instruction was French and he also studied the language in that school. French was also the language of instruction at the Catholic boarding school he attended in Beirut, as it surely was at the French Brothers' School in Ramleh. We can therefore conclude that Shoghi Effendi was both literate and fluent in the French language.

There is more evidence as to when Shoghi Effendi began his study of English. We know that Lua Getsinger taught English in 'Abdu'l-Bahá's household in Acre in 1902, when Shoghi Effendi would have been about six years old. There is no reason to doubt that he attended her lessons with the other members of the family.

Shoghi Effendi was exposed to English even earlier, while still a toddler, as Western pilgrims began in 1898 to visit 'Abdu'l-Bahá in Acre. Except for some brief periods in the early part of the century when 'Abdu'l-Bahá was confined to Acre and during the war years, the stream of pilgrims from all parts did not stop. Doubtless English was often spoken in 'Abdu'l-Bahá's home by these pilgrims. 'Abdu'l-Bahá Himself knew some English and Shoghi Effendi's mother and three maternal aunts wrote and spoke English. A Tablet of 'Abdu'l-Bahá known as 'The Seven Candles of Unity' was translated by 'Abdu'l-Bahá's daughter Munavvar Khánum. This Tablet was revealed in response to a letter left by a Scottish pilgrim, Mrs Whyte, in March 1906.[49] We may assume that the translation was also completed in 1906 and, if so, this is an indication of the level of competency achieved by at least this one daughter of 'Abdu'l-Bahá. Other translations of 'Abdu'l-Bahá's works into English by his daughters also exist. It seems 'Abdu'l-Bahá's wife did not know how to speak English at this early date, for in 1905 she remarked to an American pilgrim, Julia M. Grundy, 'I regret indeed that I cannot speak your language. You also feel your need of Persian.'[50]

From this interchange it is apparent that facility in English was considered very desirable, particularly because of all the English-speaking visitors. Being members of a household in which consummate courtesy was enjoined on all alike, the family would surely have wanted to ease their Western visitors' stay by conversing with them in their own language.

Thus, Shoghi Effendi lived in a household where English was known by members of his family and where it was frequently spoken. In addition, 'Abdu'l-Bahá received large quantities of correspondence in English from Bahá'ís in other parts of the world and His responses in Persian were often translated by secretaries who assisted Him in His home. This would have further exposed Shoghi Effendi to English. Moreover, if in 1910, as indicated in the memoirs of Fallscheer, 'Abdu'l-Bahá was already determined that Shoghi Effendi become proficient in English, He would have encouraged His grandson's acquisition of that language. It is most likely that Shoghi Effendi did study English under the Jesuits before going to the American University in Beirut, for 'Alí Nakhjavání notes that 'the Jesuits taught English as a subject, but the means of instruction was French'.[51] Shoghi Effendi worked hard at acquiring English, as his wife attests:

> From his Beirut days until practically the end of his life Shoghi Effendi had the habit of writing vocabularies and typical English phrases in notebooks. Hundreds of words and sentences have been recorded and these clearly indicate the years of careful study he put into mastering a language he loved and revelled in. For him there was no second to English.[52]

Shoghi Effendi graduated with his Bachelor of Arts degree from the American University in Beirut in May 1918. He then returned to Haifa to serve as 'Abdu'l-Bahá's translator and secretary for two years. By this time he had attained a respectable proficiency in the language which his year and a half at Oxford would only refine.

Literary Endeavours

Let us now summarize Shoghi Effendi's literary output. His translation work spanned the first 23 years of his ministry from 1921 to 1944. By 1944 the globe-encircling administrative system he had nurtured and guided had grown to the point that it took up most of his time and he was unable to find much time for translating and writing.[53]

During these 23 years, in addition to the many passages translated from the writings of Bahá'u'lláh and 'Abdu'l-Bahá which adorn Shoghi Effendi's numerous letters, Shoghi Effendi translated six book-length works, one of them a history of the early years of the religion. The five others were works of Bahá'u'lláh. The first of these was the Hidden Words. The four others were the Kitáb-i-Íqán (The Book of Certitude), 1931; Gleanings from the Writings of Bahá'u'lláh, 1935; Prayers and Meditations by Bahá'u'lláh, 1938; and Epistle to the Son of the Wolf, 1941.

The significance of the works Shoghi Effendi translated may be gleaned from this passage commenting on The Book of Certitude:

> Foremost among the priceless treasures cast forth from the billowing ocean of Bahá'u'lláh's Revelation ranks the Kitáb-i-Íqán (Book of Certitude), revealed within the space of two days and two nights, in the closing years of that period (1278 AH – 1862 AD) . . . A model of Persian prose, of a style at once original, chaste and vigorous, and remarkably lucid, both cogent in argument and matchless in its irresistible eloquence, this Book, setting forth in outline the Grand Redemptive Scheme of God, occupies a position unequalled by any work in the entire range of Bahá'í literature, except the Kitáb-i-Aqdas, Bahá'u'lláh's Most Holy Book.[54]

Shoghi Effendi's translation of the Kitáb-i-Íqán covers 257 pages.[55] He comments in a letter dated 4 July 1930, 'I feel exceedingly tired after a strenuous year of work, particularly as I have managed to add to my labours the translation of

the Íqán, which I have already sent to America.'[56] It is significant that Shoghi Effendi chose this work to translate so early
in his career. *The Book of Certitude* explains the concept of
progressive revelation, fundamental to Bahá'í theology: the
founders of the major religions come in succeeding ages;
they are not in opposition to one another, rather each brings
teachings which are the fulfilment of the former dispensation. The book also explains why the founders of all the
major religions have been persecuted.

Among the 'labours' of which Shoghi Effendi wrote was
his third translation, a challenging undertaking

> . . . which must be considered a literary masterpiece . . .
> This was the translation of the first part of the narrative
> compiled by a contemporary follower of both the Báb and
> Bahá'u'lláh known as Nabíl, which was published in 1932
> under the title of *The Dawn-Breakers . . . Nabíl's Narrative . . .*
> deserves to be counted as a classic among epic narratives in
> the English tongue. Although ostensibly a translation from
> the original Persian Shoghi Effendi may be said to have re-
> created it in English, his translation being comparable to
> Fitzgerald's rendering of Omar Khayyam's *Rubaiyat* which
> gave to the world a poem in a foreign language that in
> many ways far exceeded the merits of the original.[57]

The translated volume is 748 pages long and contains 150
photographs. It took him two years of research and eight
months to write. Of it he says, 'I have been so absorbed in
this work that I have been forced to delay my correspondence . . . I am so tired and exhausted that I can hardly
write.'[58] His capabilities as an historian are very evident in
this carefully documented chronicle. Many of the footnotes
are from French sources and were not translated into English by Shoghi Effendi, presumably because he did not have
time; they were later translated into English by someone else
and published separately in booklet form. Before Shoghi
Effendi translated this historical work, 'Abdu'l-Bahá's *A
Traveller's Narrative*, which was translated by E. G. Browne,

was the primary source of historical information on the Bábí religion. *The Dawn-Breakers* is a far more detailed history with extensive references.

Gleanings from the Writings of Bahá'u'lláh was published in 1935. It is, in Shoghi Effendi's own words, 'a selection of the most characteristic and hitherto unpublished passages from the outstanding works of the Author of the Bahá'í Revelation'.[59] The book contains 165 passages and the American edition runs to 346 pages.[60]

Prayers and Meditations by Bahá'u'lláh, a book of 339 pages and 184 selected passages,[61] elicited the following comment from a former professor of Shoghi Effendi at the American University of Beirut, Bayard Dodge: 'The translation of deep and poetic thoughts, such as those in the *Prayers and Meditations*, requires an enormous amount of hard work . . . I have told you before how much I marvel when I see the quality of English that you use.'[62]

The Epistle to the Son of the Wolf was written by Bahá'u'lláh in the final years of His life and is considered His last major work. Shoghi Effendi comments:

> Finally, mention must be made of His Epistle to Shaykh Muḥammad-Taqí, surnamed 'Ibn-i-Dhi'b' (Son of the Wolf), the last outstanding Tablet revealed by the pen of Bahá'u-'lláh, in which He calls upon that rapacious priest to repent of his acts, quotes some of the most characteristic and celebrated passages of His own writings, and adduces proofs establishing the validity of His Cause.
>
> With this book, revealed about one year prior to His ascension, the prodigious achievement as author of a hundred volumes, repositories of the priceless pearls of His Revelation, may be said to have practically terminated . . .[63]

Shoghi Effendi's translation of this work comprises 181 pages.

It is interesting to note that Shoghi Effendi wrote only one book of his own as such, *God Passes By*, published in 1944 and discussed below. Other than this and his translations, his literary work was largely in the form of letters. Shoghi Effendi's correspondence was a never-ending and onerous task that spanned the entire 36 years of his Guardianship. In its statistical report published in April 1986 the Universal House of Justice noted that it held some 11,800 letters 'of the estimated 22,500 letters to which the Guardian is known to have replied'.[64]

While by 'correspondence' one generally means letters of only a few pages, many of Shoghi Effendi's letters were extremely lengthy, including two of book length. *The Advent of Divine Justice*, comprising 91 pages, was written to the Bahá'ís of the United States and Canada in 1938 and published just before the outbreak of World War II in September 1939. A general letter to the Bahá'ís of the West, *The Promised Day is Come*, comprising 124 pages, was written in 1941 during the summer and autumn preceding the entry of the United States into World War II. Both these letters allude to America's future destiny and set 'forth the root-decay of the present day world', and propound its remedy.[65]

There are eleven compilations of Shoghi Effendi's correspondence which include several particularly important and notable letters. Among these is *The World Order of Bahá'u'lláh* containing seven letters written between 1929 and 1936: 'The World Order of Bahá'u'lláh' (10 pages); 'The World Order of Bahá'u'lláh: Further Considerations' (12 pages); 'The Goal of a New World Order' (20 pages); 'The Golden Age of the Cause of Bahá'u'lláh' (18 pages); 'America and the Most Great Peace' (24 pages); 'The Dispensation of Bahá'u'lláh' (53 pages); and 'The Unfoldment of World Civilization' (46 pages). These letters are heavily interspersed with Shoghi Effendi's translations of Bahá'í sacred texts and, of course, are considered exposition of those texts in his capacity as expounder. These letters explain the nature and goals of the new world civilization anticipated by the Bahá'ís and greatly clarify the character of the New World Order which Bahá'u'lláh declared it His mission to establish. Of particular note is the 'Dispensation of Bahá'u'lláh', published in 1934, which defines with copious references the theology of the Bahá'í Faith, explaining particularly the place of the three central figures of the religion in their relationship to God and to each other.

Mention must also be made of Shoghi Effendi's cables. He developed a style for writing cables which reads best without the usual interposing of conjunctions, prepositions, and so forth. Some of his cables are five pages in length. His wife explains:

> Shoghi Effendi developed what one might call the language of cables to such a high degree that they became a literary accomplishment. Not infrequently he sent cables the length of letters. He thought in the abbreviated form when he wrote them. It was not a question of expressing a thought in the normal style of composition and then eliminating all the words that could be left out and still convey the meaning; from the beginning he did not think those words into his text at all and thus the style is very graphic, powerful and dramatic.[66]

To illustrate this, here is a short cable written by Shoghi Effendi:

> CHEERED HEARTENED MAGNIFICENT SUCCESS TEACHING CONFERENCE. GREATLY WELCOME VALUABLE ASSISTANCE EXTENDED DISTINGUISHED TEACHER DOROTHY BAKER. INITIAL PHASE PLAN DRAWING TRIUMPHANT CLOSE. SIGNAL SERVICES RENDERED SOUND BLESSED FIRMLY KNIT WIDE AWAKE BRITISH BAHÁ'Í COMMUNITY EVOKING ADMIRATION SISTER COMMUNITIES EAST WEST SETTING STIRRING EXAMPLE RISING GENERATION CONFERRING INESTIMABLE BLESSINGS POSTERITY MERITING APPLAUSE CONCOURSE ON HIGH AUGMENTING MY DEBT GRATITUDE. PRAYING ARDENTLY SUCCESS NEWLY LAUNCHED CO-ORDINATED TEACHING PLAN SUPPLICATING RICHEST BLESSINGS NEWLY ARISEN PIONEERS DEEPEST LOVE. SHOGHI[67]

Shoghi Effendi wrote his only book, *God Passes By*, to mark the centenary of the founding of the Faith it chronicles. It is a history in the true sense of the word. It is not an event by event chronology but an analysis and synthesis of the history of the religion's heroic and formative first years and their implication for the vast panorama of human history both past and present. Shoghi Effendi also wrote a similar, though much shorter, version in Persian for the Iranian Bahá'ís.

To the above projects must be added Shoghi Effendi's editing of the *Bahá'í World* volumes, yearbooks of the Bahá'í Faith around the globe. It was a laborious undertaking for Shoghi Effendi, since a mass of detailed information had to be amassed, culled and organized. His wife gives us some idea of the difficulty of the task:

> Volume One, published in 1925 and called *Bahá'í Year Book* – which covered the period from April 1925 to April 1926 and comprised 174 pages – received its permanent title, in Volume Two, of *The Bahá'í World, A Biennial International Record*, suggested by that National Assembly and approved by Shoghi Effendi. At the time of the Guardian's passing twelve volumes had appeared, the largest running to over 1,000 pages. Although these were prepared under the supervision of the American National Assembly, published by its Publishing Committee, compiled by a staff of editors and dedicated to Shoghi Effendi, it would be more in conformity with the facts to call them Shoghi Effendi's Book. He himself acted as Editor-in-Chief; the tremendous amount of material comprised in each volume was sent to him by the American Assembly, with all photographs, before it appeared and his was the final decision as to what should go in and be omitted.[68]

This project initiated by Shoghi Effendi has been continued since his passing. Volumes 13 to 19 have been published under the auspices of the Universal House of Justice. In 1992 the volumes began to be published annually.

Interpreter and Expounder: Distinctions

Bahá'u'lláh designated His son, 'Abdu'l-Bahá, the Head of the Bahá'í Faith after His death and the Interpreter of its teachings. 'Abdu'l-Bahá was the only person authorized to interpret the writings of Bahá'u'lláh and to explain their meaning to the believers. In turn, 'Abdu'l-Bahá, in His Will and Testament, appointed Shoghi Effendi as Guardian of the Bahá'í Faith and its expounder after His death, an office Shoghi Effendi assumed in 1921. Others may interpret the Bahá'í sacred writings for themselves – and they may share these interpretations with others – but only 'Abdu'l-Bahá's interpretations, and Shoghi Effendi's after Him, have any authority. (For a discussion of the appointment of Shoghi Effendi as Guardian and expounder of the Bahá'í Faith, see Appendixes.)

At this point it is useful to explore more carefully what is meant by 'interpreter' and 'expounder' in the Bahá'í teachings. Shoghi Effendi said in a letter dated 18 December 1937 that 'the Master [a title given to 'Abdu'l-Bahá by Bahá'u'lláh] should be referred to as the interpreter of the Word and not as expounder, the former being much more precise and more faithful to the original Persian word used by Bahá'u-'lláh'.[69] David Hofman, who received this letter, comments:

> We may conclude from this, bearing in mind the station and powers of 'Abdu'l-Bahá, that the Interpreter has authority to declare both the inner and outer meaning of the sacred text, to add to it, His word being part of the Revelation itself and unchangeable. The expounder does not add to the Revelation, although his exposition and interpretation have the same validity as the text itself . . . It is clearly recognized that Shoghi Effendi made no changes and added nothing to the Revelation. He disclosed to our astonished eyes the writings by the three central figures . . . He initiated and supervised the practical application to Bahá'í affairs of directives, injunctions, laws and ordinances in the scared text, as he was guided to do.[70]

However, the distinction between these two terms 'interpreter' and 'expounder' is not always clear in the Bahá'í writings. In Shoghi Effendi's translation of the Will and Testament of 'Abdu'l-Bahá, received by the American Bahá'ís on 25 February 1922 in New York, Shoghi Effendi is named as 'the expounder of the words of God'.[71] This translation also appears in the excerpts from the Will and Testament of 'Abdu'l-Bahá found in *Bahá'í Administration*, which also includes a collection of letters from Shoghi Effendi, first published in 1928. However, in 'The Dispensation of Bahá'u'lláh', written in 1934, Shoghi Effendi translates this phrase from the Will and Testament of 'Abdu'l-Bahá as 'He is the Interpreter of the Word of God'[72] and it is this translation which is used in present translations of the Will and Testament.[73]

Thus Shoghi Effendi himself translated the original word as both 'expounder' and 'interpreter' and this might be why Bahá'ís commonly use both when referring to Shoghi Effendi. For our present purpose, however, and for the sake of clarity, the term 'expounder' will be used to refer to Shoghi Effendi as the one authorized by 'Abdu'l-Bahá in His Will and Testament to explain, clarify and apply the Bahá'í writings.

Notwithstanding this distinction, part of Shoghi Effendi's function as expounder was 'to interpret'; indeed, one of the definitions of 'to expound' is 'to interpret' – the dictionary meanings of 'expound' and 'interpret' overlap:

> **expound** 1. to set forth point by point; state in detail. 2. to explain or interpret; clarify – SYN see EXPLAIN

> **interpret** 1. to explain the meaning of; make understandable = to interpret a poem. 2. to translate (esp. oral remarks). 3. to have or show one's own understanding of the meaning of; construe = to interpret a silence as contempt. 4. to bring out the meaning of; to give one's own conception of (a work of art) as in performance or criticism. vi. to act as an interpreter; explain or translate–SYN see EXPLAIN[74]

There are some subtle differences between the two words. For example, 'to expound' has a meaning of 'to set forth point by point' and 'state in detail', which is not part of the definition of 'to interpret'. However, 'to interpret' can mean 'to show one's own understanding of' and 'to give one's own conception of'. Shoghi Effendi's duty as exegete encompasses shades of both meanings and therefore the verbs 'to expound' and 'to interpret' are used interchangeably in the present volume to imply a concept of something broader than either term.

3

The Hidden Words

The Structure of the Hidden Words

Upon Bahá'u'lláh's return to Baghdad from His self-imposed exile in the mountains of Sulaymáníyyih there ensued a period of particular fecundity in His writing during which His two most important works after the Kitáb-i-Aqdas (Most Holy Book) were penned. Shoghi Effendi in his book *God Passes By* writes:

> Next to this unique repository of inestimable treasures [Kitáb-i-Íqán] must rank that marvellous collection of gem-like utterances, the 'Hidden Words' with which Bahá'u'lláh was inspired, as He paced, wrapped in His meditations, the banks of the Tigris.[75]

The Hidden Words (Kalimát-i-Maknúnih) were written about 1858. Bahá'u'lláh states that the first verses were written in a Tablet and additional verses penned at various times.[76]

The Hidden Words is an ethical and mystical work, unique in Bahá'u'lláh's corpus in its form and composition. It is relatively short and is in two parts, the first in Arabic and second in Persian. This examination of the Hidden Words focuses primarily on the Arabic section but it is necessary to describe briefly the whole work. Although the Arabic section can stand alone, as indeed can each of its separate verses, the book is one complete work, beginning with a Prologue and ending with an Epilogue, united in substance and form.

The Arabic Hidden Words opens with an invocation: 'He is the Glory of Glories', followed by a Prologue and 71 discrete parts or verses. Each verse is introduced by an address such as 'O Son of Man' or 'O Son of Spirit'. The Arabic Hidden Words, excluding the initial addresses, vary in length from two lines in English to a modest paragraph. The Persian section also begins with an invocation: 'In the Name of the Lord of Utterance, the Mighty'. However, this section has no Prologue and it is quite apparent that the Persian section merely continues the overall piece. At the end, however, is an Epilogue which closes the whole work. The Persian section is longer than the Arabic, with 82 entries, which tend to be longer than the Arabic ones.

The Hidden Words was written as a guidebook for erring humanity, to lead humankind along the spiritual path. Bahá'u'lláh clearly indicates His purpose in the Prologue:

> This is that which hath descended from the realm of glory, uttered by the tongue of power and might, and revealed unto the Prophets of old. We have taken the inner essence thereof and clothed it in the garment of brevity, as a token of grace unto the righteous, that they may stand faithful unto the Covenant of God, may fulfil in their lives His trust, and in the realm of spirit obtain the gem of Divine virtue.[77]

Thus Bahá'u'lláh claims the work to be a distillation of the essence of all the religious teachings of the past, written in a new and concise form 'for the reorientation of the minds of men, the edification of their souls and the rectification of their conduct'.[78] The concept of distillation claimed for the work's content is also a prime feature of its structure. Each of the Hidden Words is the epitome of conciseness, containing vast ideas in very terse, pithy stanzas.

Thematically, numerous strands wind themselves intricately through the broader tapestry. They are like an arabesque, weaving in and out without an abrupt beginning or end. Some stanzas in proximity address a certain theme, such as love (Arabic nos. 3–10), faultfinding (Arabic nos. 26–9), death (Arabic nos. 31–4), martyrdom (Arabic nos. 45–57) and tribulation (Arabic nos. 48–53). However, in stanzas dealing ostensibly with one subject, other themes enter, are picked up, then disappear only to re-appear later in another stanza, giving the work a rich texture. Attempts to break down the Hidden Words into thematic categories have not been very successful, the work itself resisting such compartmentalization. The work is far too complex to allow – even with effort exerted over much time – anything but a loose explanation of the relation of theme to structure, or progression and rationale of its intricate and interwoven ideas. Indeed, Shoghi Effendi himself states that 'The Hidden Words have no sequence. They are jewel-like thoughts cast out of the mind of the Manifestation of God to admonish and counsel men . . .'[79]

The Hidden Words of Bahá'u'lláh is a unique literary form in both Persian and Arabic letters. It is, of course, influenced by earlier literary models, beginning with the Qur'án in the seventh century, and by both Persian and Arabic literature. Specific literary influences on the Hidden Words will be examined in the next sections.

The Influence of the Qur'án on the Hidden Words

The Qur'án has from its inception been regarded by Muslims as the highest form of the written word and the grammatical, stylistic and literary model for written Arabic. So important is the Qur'án and the language in which it was written that when the Islamic Empire spread beyond the confines of the Arabian Peninsula and encompassed lands, such as Persia, where other languages were spoken, Arabic retained its primacy as the medium of the sciences, theology and jurisprudence.

The Qur'án is considered a miracle, given to Muḥammad by God through the archangel Gabriel. The reverence accorded it and high regard in which it is held are unparalleled in the history of Islam, which dates from the Migration (Hegira) of 622 AD. Muslims consider the Qur'án to be inimitable and the loftiest form of written expression.

The Qur'án was revealed over a period of some 23 years. It was written down in the days of Muḥammad but it was essentially a memorized work, kept in the minds of the early believers. Abu Bakr, the second Caliph, reputedly compiled a complete Qur'án with all its suras after many of those who had memorized the book in full were killed in battle. Uthman, the third Caliph, was aware that there were some variant readings of the Qur'án and compiled an authoritative version which is still in use over 1,400 years later.[80]

Structurally the Qur'án and the Hidden Words are quite different. The Qur'án is composed of suras, or chapters, which are made up of verses. The whole book is in Arabic. The Hidden Words is composed not of chapters but of short, individual meditations; it is in two languages, Arabic and Persian.

There are, however, some similarities between the two works. A feature common to both is that discrete stanzas can be lifted out of the whole and still retain their integrity of meaning and artistry. That is, each can be broken down into the smallest of units, each unit functioning independently of the rest of the text. Of course, this is also true for many of the verses of poetry in the Bible, such as the Psalms. However, because of its structure of short discrete parts, this is particularly true of the Hidden Words. Bahá'u'lláh was very familiar with the Qur'án, and although I do not suggest there was a direct influence of the one on the other, Bahá'u-'lláh must have been aware of this characteristic.

We will now examine two features of the Qur'án that have clearly influenced the form of – and are also found in – the Hidden Words: *saj'* or rhymed prose, and parallelism.

Saj'

Muḥammad was not at all readily accepted as the Prophet by His fellow countrymen; and His book, which was in prose, necessitated a strong defence since not only did people refute His claim as to its divine origins but they were unable to classify its literary status,[81] as shown in the following passage from the Qur'án:

> That is indeed the speech of an illustrious messenger.
> It is not poet's speech – little is it that ye believe!
> Nor diviner's speech – little is it that ye remember!
> It is a revelation from the Lord of the Worlds.[82]

As can be seen, Muḥammad was accused of being both poet and sorcerer or soothsayer, uttering incantations. This is due to the style of the poetic prose, call *saj'*, which is used in the early short Meccan suras of the Qur'án:

> [*Saj'*] introduces the basic poetic ingredients of rhyme and rhythm into prose without actually transforming it into equal-footed lines. A symmetry of expression is achieved by use of lexical devices such as synonyms, antonyms, and homonyms giving prose an architectural plasticity and rendering it memorable.[83]

Saj' has strong features of rhymed and metred verse, which led to the confusion of Muḥammad with a poet, but it is not poetry. Rather, it is formalized and very stylized poetic prose:

> In pagan times it is supposed to have been the mode of expression in dignified discourses, challenges, harangues and orations. It was also the form in which the oracular saying and decisions of the *kahana*, the soothsayers or diviners . . . were expressed.[84]

A form of *saj'* with this purpose was in use when Muḥammad employed it in the Qur'án and thus He was accused of sorcery. Despite the criticism of Muḥammad's detractors, the exquisite use of *saj'* in the Qur'án has had a profound influence on Arabic and Persian letters.

The early Meccan suras, composed before the Hegira,

show a stronger, more sustained use of *saj'* than is apparent in the later suras. The Meccans suras are more mystical and are concerned with man's relationship to God. These are the suras of Muḥammad's early prophetic mission when He was urging His compatriots to heed His words and acknowledge God's revelation. His later suras date from the Medina period and deal with political, legal and other questions facing the newborn Muslim community. The verses of these suras are longer and do not have internal rhyme, nor do they use similar rhythms. However, the last word of a verse does usually rhyme with the last word of the preceding and following verses.[85]

The early Meccan suras in which the use of *saj'* is most evident are much shorter than the later suras, some of which run to many pages. The shortest Meccan suras are only four or five lines long, while others run to a page or two or three.

The *saj'* makes abundant use of internal and end rhythm and rhyme. By way of example, let us look at Mankind ('*N-nás* 114:1-6), an early Meccan sura, the phonetic transliteration of which is followed by an English translation:

bismilláhi 'r-rahmáni 'r-rahím

1. qul a'udhu birabbi 'n-nás
2. maliki 'n-nás
3. aláhi 'n-nás
4. min sharri 'l-waswás 'l-khannás
5. alladhi yuwaswisu fi sudúri 'n-nás
6. min al-jinnati wan-nás

In the name of Alláh, the Beneficent, the Merciful.

1. Say: I seek refuge in the Lord of mankind.
2. The King of mankind,
3. The God of mankind,
4. From the evil of the sneaking whisperer,
5. Who whispereth in the hearts of mankind,
6. Of the jinn and of mankind.[86]

The end rhyme repeats itself in each of the lines above, excluding the invocation 'In the name of Alláh, the Beneficent, the Merciful', which opens each sura of the Qur'án and is not part of any of the rhyme schemes. Thus *'n-nás* is the end rhyme of each line of this sura. There is also internal rhyme, as in *'l-waswás* of line 4 which rhymes with *'l-khannás*, the word following it in the same line. Of course, it also rhymes with all of the end rhymes.

The transliteration above indicates a readily discernible rhythm which is even more apparent when the sura is recited or chanted. For example, lines 2 and 3 have the same rhythm, and the second half of line 1 also has the same rhythm as lines 2 and 3 with three open syllables in the word preceding *'n-nás*. In lines 4 and 5 *min sharri 'l-waswás* has the same rhythm as *fi sudúri 'n-nás* of line 5, and they also rhyme, which is a good example of the intricate overlapping of these features. There is also a general rhythm which is not bound by any particular schemata or rules but can be felt as a powerful and seductive influence.

Alliteration, assonance and consonance are also apparent in this sura and are a feature of *saj'*. An example of alliteration, the repetition of initial sounds in adjacent words or syllables, is found in lines 2, 4 and 6 of the above verse: all begin with an 'm' sound. Consonance, the repetition of consonants, is strongly felt in lines 4 and 5 with the repetition of the 'w' and 's' sounds of *'l-waswás* and *yuwaswisu*; the 's' sound is given further thrust in *sudúr*, also of line 5. Of course, the rhyme entails the 's' of *'n-nás*, further illustrating the intensity and complexity of *saj'* in its finest expression. Assonance, the repetition of vowels, also strongly appears in the end rhyme of *'n-nás* and in the internal rhyme of *'l-waswás* of line 4. One can find several more examples of these various elements of *saj'* in this sura and others.

We now turn to the Hidden Words. The Hidden Words has its inception in the Islamic literary tradition and, like the early Quranic suras, is written in *saj'*. Let us look at a typical passage:

43

ya 'bna 'l-insán

a rakada fi barri 'l-'amá	1
thumma asra'a fi maidani 's-samá	2
lan tajidu 'r-ráhatan	3
illa bil-khudú'i li amriná	4
wat-tawádu'i li wajhimá	5

O Son of Man!
Wert thou to speed through the immensity of space and traverse the expanse of heaven, yet thou wouldst find no rest save in submission to Our command and humbleness before Our Face.[87]

Like the Quranic suras, each Hidden Word opens with an introductory salutation. As with the sura 'N-nás, each line of the Hidden Word has the same end rhyme, except for line 3, which divides the two halves of this passage into symmetrical elements. Thus lines 1, 2, 4 and 5 end with an 'a' sound. Lines 1 and 2 have the further rhymes of *amá* while lines 4 and 5 rhyme on *iná*.

The rhyme in this Hidden Word is not as close as that of the sura above but there is no doubt that the rhyme is deliberate and in the style of *saj'*. Further, the final words of lines 1 and 2, and 4 and 5, rhyme in their accenting. Thus *'il-'amá* rhymes with *'s-samá*, and *li amriná* rhymes with *li wajhimá*. There is also internal rhyme. For example, the *fi* of lines 1 and 2 rhyme and the phrases *illa bil-khudú'i* and *wat-tawádu'i* have a general rhyme to them, although it is not exact. Also, *rakada* of line 1 rhymes with *asra'a* of line 2.

The rhyme, of course, is best appreciated when heard. However, even in reading the transliteration, or much better, the Arabic, we sense a strong rhythm. Lines 1 (with nine syllables) and 2 (with eleven syllables) rhyme very closely and have the same stress patterns. Lines 4 and 5 have essentially the same rhythmic pattern, with line 4 having ten syllables and line 5 having nine, again with the same rhythm.

Alliteration is very evident throughout. The *ra* of *rakada* in line 1 has a counterpoint in the *ra* of *asra'a* of line 2. The *fí* of lines 1 and 2 and *li* of lines 4 and 5 are alliterative. In line 5 the *wa* sound appears twice in *wat-tawádu'i* and once in *wajhiná*. As for consonance, the 't' sound appears in every line except the last; the 't' sound appears twice in line 3 and once in line 5; the 'd' sound repeats itself in lines 2, 3, 4 and 5; and the 'h' is in lines 3, 4 and 5. Finally, assonance is most evident in the end rhymes with the long and short 'a', which is the most repeated sound in this particular Hidden Word, showing itself in all except five words.

The use of *saj'* is found throughout the Hidden Words and is readily apparent. For this reason the Hidden Words lend themselves easily to chanting or recitation. It is accepted by all authorities that the Qur'án is the literary work responsible for the introduction of *saj'* into prose works; the Hidden Words is in the literary tradition of Arabic letters inspired by the Qur'án, although it has its own, unique features.

Parallelism

All ancient Near Eastern poetry is based on parallelism, found both in the Bible and the Qur'án. It appears frequently in the Hidden Words. By parallelism is meant the repetition and juxtaposition of similar ideas and syntactical and stylistic elements to lend intensity and emotional appeal. A comparison of parallelism as it is found in the Qur'án with the parallelism of the Hidden Words illustrates how the Hidden Words was influenced by the Qur'án.

'The Disbelievers' is a Meccan sura (109:1-6) 'revealed at a time when the idolaters had asked the Prophet to compromise in matters of religion':

In the name of Allah, the Beneficent, the Merciful.

1. Say: O disbelievers!
2. I worship not that which ye worship.
3. Nor worship ye that which I worship.

4. And I shall not worship that which ye worship.
5. Nor will ye worship that which I worship.
6. Unto you your religion, and unto me my religion.[88]

In this sura the parallelism is very symmetrical and is evident in all but the first line. Again, we exclude the invocation 'In the name of Alláh, the Beneficent, the Merciful' from this examination of the parallel features of the sura. However, it must be mentioned that this invocation, by appearing at the beginning of all but one of the suras of the Qur'án, itself acts as a parallel feature, tying together each individual sura into the fabric of the whole and also uplifting each sura and intensifying it.

Lines 2 and 3 of this sura are synonymously parallel and repeat the same thought while employing chiasmas, as indicated by the inverted order. Each is a negative statement in the present tense using the verb 'worship' but inverting the pronouns. Thus 'I worship not' of line 2 is paralleled by 'Nor worship ye' of line 3. The phrase 'that which ye worship' of line 2 is parallelled by 'that which I worship' of line 3. Syntactically they are the same except that line 3 inverts the negation of line 2; thus, 'I worship not' of line 2 becomes 'Nor worship ye' of line 3. Lines 4 and 5 behave in the same way; they are also synonymously parallel chiastic statements. Both are in the future tense and use the same verb, 'worship'. Except for 'And' in line 4, these two lines parallel each other exactly, as did lines 2 and 3. Each is a negative statement. 'I shall not worship' of line 4 parallels 'Nor will ye worship' of line 5. The phrase 'that which ye worship' of line 4 parallels 'that which I worship' of line 5, except that the pronouns are reversed. Lines 2 and 3 also parallel lines 4 and 5 in all the elements observed except for the 'And' of line 4, which breaks the sura into two parts and emphasizes its meaning. In line 6 the independent clause 'Unto you your religion' is antithetically parallel to the independent clause 'unto me my religion'. Again, the 'and' which balances and unites these two statements emphasizes the meaning of the line. Lines 1 and 6, though not parallel units, do act as address and final statement: 'Say: O disbelievers! . . . Unto you your religion, and unto me my religion.' They enclose the parallel lines of 2 through 5 and highlight the parallel elements. This sura is a good example of the extent to which parallelism is used in the Qur'án, most notably in the early Meccan suras which are the more poetic and in which *saj'* is also especially evident.

The two following passages from the Arabic illustrate the employment of parallelism as a feature of the Hidden Words:

35. O Son of Man!
Sorrow not save that thou art far from Us. Rejoice not save that thou art drawing near and returning unto Us.

50. O Son of Man!
If adversity befall thee not in My path, how canst thou walk in the ways of them that are content with my pleasure? And if trials afflict thee not in thy longing to meet Me, how wilt thou attain the light in thy love for My beauty?

The address 'O Son of Man', which is used in each of these Hidden Words, is excluded from an analysis of the parallel features of the text. However, since each Hidden Word opens with such an address, this parallel feature acts in much the same way as the invocation 'In the name of Alláh, the Beneficent, the Merciful' which opens the suras of the Qur'án. These addresses unify, emphasize and highlight the work. In Hidden Word Arabic 35 we find two antithetically parallel negative statements: 'Sorrow not save that thou art far from Us' and 'Rejoice not save that thou art drawing near and returning unto Us'. The second statement uses two verbs – 'art drawing near and returning' – instead of the one verb of the first statement – 'art far' – and is thus an instance of incomplete parallelism with compensation, that is, the elements of the second grouping of words is not exactly matched by the first. The prepositional phrase which concludes the first line – 'from Us' – parallels the prepositional phrase of the second line – 'unto Us' – except that each has the opposite meaning. However the two verbs of the second line – 'drawing near and returning' – are both parallel to each other. Even in this short Hidden Word the parallelism is very apparent.

Hidden Word Arabic 50 is composed of two synonymous or repetitively parallel, anaphoric interrogative statements, both beginning with the word 'If'. Each sentence begins with a conditional phrase beginning with 'If' and is in the negative. 'If adversity befall thee not in My path' of the first sentence parallels 'If trials afflict thee not in thy longing to meet Me' of the second. 'Adversity' has the same meaning as 'trials', and 'befall' and 'afflict' are essentially the same. 'In My path' of line 1 matches 'in thy longing to meet Me' of line 2, as it stands to reason that if one travels on the path towards God, one longs to meet Him. The interrogative, anaphoric clause in each sentence of this Hidden Word starts with the word 'how' and each parallels the other. Thus, 'how canst thou walk in the ways of them that are content with My pleasure' parallels 'how wilt thou attain the light in thy love for My beauty'. Each line asks a similar question. If one walks in the ways of them that are content with God's pleasure, they will attain the light in their love for His beauty. There is a clear parallelism here that shows itself throughout the Hidden Words, and the meaning, too, has parallel implications, as was also observed in the sura above.

Parallelism is a literary device particularly used in poetry and poetic prose. The above examples from the Hidden Words and the Qur'án are striking illustrations. In the Qur'án, as noted above, it appears primarily in the poetic Meccans suras in which *saj'* is also heavily used. It is found in almost every Arabic Hidden Word. Bahá'u'lláh was intimately familiar with the Qur'án and its literary characteristics. His abundant use in the Hidden Words of this Quranic feature of parallelism invested His book with Quranic overtones and identified it as a work of scripture. Had Bahá'u-

'lláh departed from this model, His readers may not have recognized the work as scripture.

Literary Influence of the Aḥadíth Qudsíyyih 'Sacred Traditions' on the Hidden Words

The Traditions of Islam (ḥadíth, pl. aḥadíth) are the reported sayings and actions of the Prophet Muḥammad:

> The Prophet's pious followers . . . endeavoured to preserve for the edification and instruction of the community everything that he said, both in public and in private, regarding the practice of the religious obligations prescribed by him, the conduct of life in general, and social behaviour . . .[89]

Next to the Qur'án the Ḥadíth has had the greatest influence on theology and Islamic jurisprudence as it provided guidance on problems and situations not specifically dealt with in the Qur'án. Each of these traditions begins with a chain of reporters which reputedly determines the veracity of the tradition. The transmission of the tradition, isnád in Arabic, is cited before giving the text of the tradition; thus, so and so heard from so and so who heard from so and so who heard from a companion of the Prophet who saw the Prophet do a certain thing or say a particular thing. The tradition is ultimately supposed to be traced back to Muḥammad. During the first two centuries of Islam, spurious traditions were created to justify competing political and theological positions, as well as to provide edification and even entertainment. This state of affairs greatly complicated the identification and compilation of authentic traditions by Muslim scholars. Nonetheless, there are several compilers of these traditions whose collections are considered reliable by orthodox Muslims and have influenced jurisprudence for centuries. A typical example, without all the complications of its transmission, follows:

On the authority of Ibn Mas'ud (may God be pleased with him) who said that the Messenger of God (the peace and blessings of God be upon him) said:

The spilling of the blood of a Muslim is not lawful except in one of three cases: The married person who commits adultery, the life taken in exchange for a life and the apostate who leaves his religious community (Islam).[90]

A Ḥadíth deals primarily with legal questions directed to Muḥammad and with what the Prophet did in certain circumstances such as eating, greeting friends and making decisions.[91]

The Aḥadíth Qudsíyyih or Sacred Traditions differ from the Traditions in several ways. The major difference is that God speaks to man, and not Muḥammad:

Ḥadíth Kudsí (sacred, or holy tradition), also called *hadíth iláhí*, or *rabbání* (divine tradition), is a class of traditions which give words spoken by God, as distinguished from *hadíth nabawí* (prophetical tradition) which gives the words of the Prophet. Although *hadíth kudsí* is said to contain God's words, it differs from the Kur'an which was revealed through the medium of Gabriel, is inimitable, is recited in the *salat* prescribed daily prayer, and may not be touched or recited by the ceremonially unclean. Ḥadíth Kudsí does not necessarily come through Gabriel, but may have come through inspiration (*ilhám*), or in a dream . . . The words are not God's exact words, but express their meaning. They may not be used in *salat*, and there is no harm if one touches them when ceremonially unclean. Disbelief in the Kur'an is infidelity, but this does not apply to *hadíth kudsí*. When quoting a *hadíth kudsí* one must not say simply, 'God said' as when quoting the Kur'an, but either 'God's messenger said in what is related from his Lord', or 'God most high said in what God's messenger related from Him'.[92]

As can be seen, these Traditions are considered sacred because they represent what God has said directly to man.

While the Ḥadíth deals with everyday life in a practical fashion, the Sacred Traditions are mystical in tone and address man's mystical relationship with God. The Sacred Traditions had a profound influence on the development of Sufism, the mystical movement in Islam. Certain of the Sacred Traditions are the cornerstones of the theological edifice of Sufistic belief. The following Sacred Tradition is presented as an example:

> He who seeks Me finds Me and he who finds Me loves Me, and he who loves Me, I love him, and he whom I love, I kill, and he whom I kill, I am his blood-price.[93]

This Ḥadíth Qudsí is mystical in tone and nature and intimately addresses the relationship between the lover seeking God and God's love for him. Several of Bahá'u'lláh's Hidden Words are intentional allusions to certain Ḥadíth Qudsí. Let us now compare the following Ḥadíth Qudsí with two of the Hidden Words, Arabic 3 and 4.

> I was a hidden treasure and desired to be known, therefore I created man so that I might be known.

> 3. O Son of Man!
> Veiled in My immemorial being and in the ancient eternity of My essence, I knew My love for thee; therefore I created thee, have engraved on thee Mine image and revealed to thee My beauty.

> 4. O Son of Man!
> I loved thy creation, hence I created thee. Wherefore, do thou love Me, that I may name thy name and fill thy soul with the spirit of life.

These two Hidden Words reiterate the central idea of the Ḥadíth Qudsí and then elaborate on it. In the Ḥadíth Qudsí God states that He was 'a hidden treasure' and, therefore, created man so that He might be known. In other words, the reason for creation is revealed. Hidden Word Arabic 3 also states that God was hidden – He was 'veiled' in His 'immemorial being' – and then tells us that, therefore, He created man. The Hidden Word goes on to say that God's image was 'engraved' upon man and His beauty revealed to him. Thus, the Hidden Word takes the central idea further and adds to it. In Hidden Word Arabic 4 we are told that God created man because He 'loved' his 'creation'. Again, the allusion to the above Ḥadíth Qudsí is unmistakable but is not as close as with Hidden Word Arabic 3. The reference to the Ḥadíth Qudsí hinges on the idea of why God created man and God's intention regarding man's creation before man came to be. It is in the first line of Hidden Word Arabic 4 that we make the connection: 'I loved thy creation, hence I created thee.' However, Hidden Word Arabic 4 has the same relationship to Hidden Word Arabic 3 as Hidden Word Arabic 3 has to the Ḥadíth Qudsí above; Arabic 4 elaborates on Arabic 3 just as Arabic 3 elaborates on the Ḥadíth Qudsí. We can see that these contiguous Hidden Words are not accidentally positioned but are intended to be in a progression. Hidden Word Arabic 4 takes the central idea of why God created man – 'I loved thy creation, hence I created thee' – and then adds to the love motif introduced in Arabic 3 by naming love as the reason for creation. The theme of love is elaborated upon by God asking man to love Him in order that He may name his name and fill his soul 'with the spirit of life'. If the Ḥadíth Qudsí above and Hidden Words Arabic 3 and 4 are read in the order presented, the elaboration of the central theme and building upon it and then re-elaborating and rebuilding are very evident. This particular Ḥadíth Qudsí is very well known and Bahá'u'lláh is well aware of the relationship that will be drawn between His work and the Aḥadíth Qudsíyyih. Thus, in one sense, Bahá'u'lláh draws on the Arabic literary tradition to which the Aḥadíth Qudsíyyih belong to demonstrate His skill and knowledge and to make a religious connection between the two bodies of work. Only some of the Hidden Words refer to the Sacred Traditions but there are examples among both the Arabic and Persian passages.

As has been stated, the speaker in the Aḥadíth Qudsíyyih is, ostensibly God; Muḥammad is merely the mouthpiece. This is also true of the Hidden Words: the speaker is God, not Bahá'u'lláh. This feature, by itself, ties the Hidden Words unequivocally to the Aḥadíth Qudsíyyih as there is not even a remote counterpart to this in the rest of Arabo-Persian literature. The implications of this audacious comparison were not lost on the Muslims, who view the likening of Bahá'u'lláh to Muḥammad as a heresy. Since Bahá'u'lláh was soon to declare Himself to be the latest messenger from God after Muḥammad, we have here an instance of the use of a literary device to make a theological statement of broad implications.

Let us now turn to the addresses which open each of the Hidden Words, both Persian and Arabic, and which have a counterpart in the Sacred Traditions. These vocative addresses appear in many of the Aḥadíth Qudsíyyih, although not all. The following two Sacred Traditions, which have counterparts in the Hidden Words, have the vocative address:

> . . . O My servants! I have forbidden oppression to Myself and have made it unlawful to you, therefore be not an oppressor one to another . . . O My servants! It is by your deeds that I take account of you and in accordance with them do I recompense you. Therefore, let him who meets with a good reward give praise to God, but he who does not meet with a good reward, let him blame no one but himself.[94]

> . . . O Son of Adam! Spend upon (my creatures) that I may spend upon thee.[95]

The vocative addresses, so frequently found in the Sacred Traditions, also appear in the Qur'án, but not nearly so often. In contrast, each Hidden Words without exception begins with such an address. This use of the vocative address in the Hidden Words is, in my estimation, also a referent to the Aḥadíth Qudsíyyih and is intentionally used to indicate that the work is on the same level as the Sacred Traditions. Again, by His use of this device, Bahá'u'lláh's claim to be a mouthpiece for the Deity would be obvious to someone schooled in Arabo-Persian letters.

Sufism and the Hidden Words

Sufism is the mystical movement in Islam which began in the eighth century as a reaction to the worldliness increasingly characterizing the Muslim community. The movement was initially marked by an ascetic impulse to flee this world though still living in it. Thus the Sufis are thought to take their name from the wool or *sub* garments they wore in preference to the rich brocades of the worldly. Many movements have influenced Sufi doctrine including Christianity, Hellenism, Gnosticism, Buddhism and Pantheism.[96] Sufis are, however, Muslim and trace their theology to the mystic verses of the Qur'án such as Sura 50:51, 'We indeed created man; and We know what his soul whispers within him and We are nearer to him than the jugular vein'; and Sura 55:26, 'All that dwells upon the earth is perishing, yet still abides the Face of thy Lord, majestic, splendid.'[97]

The Sufis' essential quest is for a return to God and a mystical reunion with Him. They postulate that the soul was with God before it was born into this world and separated from Him. The seeker, or lover, must pass through several stages of existence in his search for the Lost Beloved and reunion with Him. This concept of union is pantheistic in that God is thought to be everywhere and in all things, and yet He is hidden. All created things mirror His attributes and, at the same time, conceal His Beauty. A quality of beauty is its desire to become known in creation and, therefore, creation comes into being. The Sufi seeks ultimately to be united with God whose habitation above all is in the heart of man; when this happens, *fana'* (extinction) of self occurs and the seeker becomes merged with God Himself. This doctrine of the merging of man with God or, as orthodox Muslims contended, 'joining partners with God', which is forbidden in the Qur'án, led to the accusation of blasphemy against the Persian mystic Hallaj, who exclaimed in mystic rapture, 'I am the Truth', for which he was executed in 922 AD in Baghdad. Afterwards an attempt was made to reconcile Sufism with orthodox Muslim theology.

The influence of Sufism on Persian literature was enormous, far greater than on Arabic letters. In Persia the symbolism of the Sufis was borrowed for literary works, especially poetry, and was the hallmark of the great Persian mystic poets, Sana'i, Hafiz and Rumi, to name a few.

The first Sufi compositions in Persian are from the eleventh century, following the renaissance of the Persian language after political independence under the tenth century Saffarids and Samanids, when modern Persian emerged from the old Pahlavi just as English emerged from Anglo-Saxon. Prior to this the language of choice for literary endeavour was Arabic. The themes of this new Persian Sufi literature were of the lover seeking the Beloved and desiring reunion with Him. The Arabic poetic forms of the *qasida*, 'ancient ode of Arabia', and the *ghazal*, 'erotic love poem', were borrowed and further developed in Persian poetry. The imagery of sensual poetry dealing with the earthly beloved was used to describe the seeker and his love and yearning for God. In addition, the newly-invented *roba'i* 'quatrain' was first used at this time for mystical expression. Bacchanalian imagery was borrowed from the wine poetry of the famous Arab poet Abu Nuwas and was used in Sufi literature to describe the intoxication of the lover with the Beloved, employing symbols such as the tavern, cup-bearer and the goblet. The first major mystical Persian poet was Sana'i who died about 1140. In addition to the above poetical forms, he developed the *mathnavi* 'rhyming couplet' for use in mystical instruction; and in this tradition follow the great Persian mystic poets Attar, Hafiz, Rumi and Jami, to name a few, whose works are unrivalled in any world literature.[98]

An extensive symbolism developed around the themes of Sufism with which Persian mystic poetry was imbued. To understand this poetry one must be able to apply the appropriate meaning for these tropes. By way of example, the following are presented:

> *Rukh* (face, cheek): the revelation of Divine Beauty in Attributes of Grace, e.g. the Gracious, the Clement, the Lifegiving, the Guide, the Bountiful; Light; Divine Reality . . .

> *Khál* (mole): the point of Real Unity, which is concealed and is therefore represented as black . . .

> *Chashm* (eye): God's beholding His servants and this aptitudes . . .

> *Sharab* (wine): ecstatic experience due to the revelation of the True Beloved, destroying the foundations of reason.

> *Saqi* (wine-bearer): Reality, as loving to manifest itself in every form that is revealed.

> *Jám* (cup): the revelations of (Divine) Acts . . .

> *Kharábát* (tavern): Pure Unity (*wahdat*), undifferentiated and unqualified.

> *Kharábátí* (tavern-haunter): the true lover who is freed from the chains of discrimination, knowing that all acts, and the qualities of all things, are obliterated in the Divine Acts and Qualities.[99]

As is readily apparent from these few examples, one must understand the symbolic meaning of these tropes in order to decipher the import of Sufi mystic poetry. Some poets, however, used the symbolism to allude to both divine and profane loves or to praise both courtly patron and divine Provider, or they may not have intended reference to the divine at all. Those poets, such as Rumi, who are known to have spoken only of the divine Beloved, can be read without conjecture about the subject of the poem.

Persian literature, then, adopted and developed Sufi themes and symbolism to a superlative degree in a refined and sophisticated tradition which reached its apogee in the thirteenth century. Even when the quality of Persian letters, on the whole, declined in later centuries, the symbolism remained.

The Persian Hidden Words reflect Sufi symbolism and themes that are representative of Persian literature. For example, Sufi themes are evident in the Hidden Words Persian 4 and 36:

4. O Son of Justice!
Whither can a lover go but to the land of his beloved? and what seeker findeth rest away from his heart's desire? To the true lover reunion is life, and separation is death. His breast is void of patience and his heart hath no peace. A myriad lives he would forsake to hasten to the abode of his beloved.

36. O Son of Dust!
The wise are they that speak not unless they obtain a hearing, even as the cup-bearer, who proffereth not his cup till he findeth a seeker and the lover who crieth not out from the depths of his heart gazeth upon the beauty of his beloved. Wherefore sow the seeds of wisdom and knowledge in the pure soil of the heart, and keep them hidden, till the hyacinths of divine wisdom spring from the heart and not from mire and clay.

Both of these Hidden Words deal with themes discussed above. In Hidden Word Persian 4 the theme of the lover seeking the beloved and desiring reunion with Him is pictured as 'life' while separation is pictured as 'death'. For the Sufi mystic, too, there is no 'patience' or 'peace' except in 'the abode of his beloved'. There is no doubt that insofar as the literary tradition is concerned, Sufi themes which long ago became part of the mystic's mode of expression are called into play here and must surely evoke a long history of literary associations in one versed in Persian literature.

Hidden Word Persian 36 uses a simile – 'even as the cup-bearer, who proffereth not his cup till he findeth a seeker' – which has the familiar images in Persian literature of the cup and cup-bearer, here referring to 'the wise' who 'speak not unless they obtain a hearing'. Though one could read in the usual Sufi definitions of the symbols for the cup and cup-bearer and obtain a reasonable reading, yet it is not the only reading. Nor is it necessary to use this 'plug-in system' of tropes in order to make sense of the text. I question a rigid symbolism in the Hidden Words. However, undoubt-edly, Bahá'u'lláh makes use of the association of mystical vistas which such a reference would elicit in the reader. And again in Hidden Word Persian 4 we find the theme of the lover seeking the beloved, here yearning to gaze upon his beauty.

Thus as in Persian literature, there are referents to Sufi themes and symbolism in the Persian Hidden Words. How-ever, the Arabic Hidden Words also reflect these themes. It may have been observed that Hidden Words Arabic 3 and 4 discussed above have a Sufistic theme: the cause of creation is God's love of man before his creation and His wish to manifest His beauty.

Let us now examine two other Hidden Words, Arabic 35 and 61, for other Sufi themes.

35. O Son of Man!
Sorrow not save that thou art far from Us. Rejoice not save that thou art drawing near and returning unto Us.

61. O Son of Man!
Ascend unto My heaven, that thou mayest obtain the joy of reunion, and from the chalice of imperishable glory quaff the peerless wine.

The theme of reunion with God is clearly indicated in Hidden Word Arabic 35 in the line, 'Rejoice not save that thou art drawing near and returning unto Us'. This same theme also appears in Hidden Word Arabic 61 in 'the joy of reunion'; in this Hidden Word are two more symbols, 'chalice' and 'wine'. If we substitute the definitions of the symbols 'cup' and 'wine' as described above, we get the following:

> Ascend unto My heaven, that thou mayest obtain the joy of reunion, and from the 'revelations of (Divine) Acts' of imperishable glory quaff the peerless 'ecstatic experience due to the revelation of the True Beloved, destroying the foundations of reason'.

This is certainly a possible reading. I would offer, however, that mystical meditations are not confined to a 'correct' reading but are by nature open to many interpretations. What is significant here is that the influence of common symbols on Persian letters is unmistakable in these Hidden Words as well as others.

The Hidden Words, Purporting to be the 'Lost Book of Fáṭimih', as a Unique Literary Form

Bahá'u'lláh identified the Hidden Words (*Kalimát-i-Maknúnih*) with the Book of Fáṭimih (Ṣaḥífiy-i-Fáṭimiyyih).[100] The source of the ancient story of the Book of Fáṭimih is unknown. Nonetheless, from the period of its creation, the Bábís associated the Hidden Words with Fáṭimih's lost book which was said to have been revealed to her by the angel Gabriel upon the death of her father, the Prophet Muḥammad, as attested by Shoghi Effendi:

> Revealed in the year 1274 AH, partly in Persian, partly in Arabic, it was originally designated the 'Hidden Book of Fáṭimih', and was identified by its Author with the Book of that same name, believed by Shí'ah Islám to be in the

possession of the promised Qá'im, and to consist of words of consolation addressed by the angel Gabriel, at God's command, to Fáṭimih, and dictated to the Imám 'Alí, for the sole purpose of comforting her in her hour of bitter anguish after the death of her illustrious Father.[101]

The Shí'í branch of Islam, in which tradition Bahá'u'lláh arose and which was dominant in Persia, as it still is today, holds that the successor to the Prophet Muḥammad should have rightfully been 'Alí, His son-in-law and the husband of Fáṭimih, and after him the twelve Imáms who carried authority to interpret the Qur'án. The Twelfth Imám disappeared in the fourth century AH (tenth century AD) and was expected to return in the fullness of time as the promised Qá'im. Twelver Shí'ís (some early Shí'í sects do not accept all twelve Imáms, although the vast majority of Shí'ís are 'Twelvers', who do) believe the Hidden Book of Fáṭimih, which was handed down from one Imám to the next, to be in the possession of the hidden Twelfth Imám. The Twelfth Imám is also supposed to have two other books which comprise 'the Books' as well as 'the divine light', 'the knowledge' and 'the weapons' (sword, spear and chain-mail passed along to 'Alí by Muḥammad).[102]

The book of Fáṭimih, also called Mushaf Fatima(h), is described in *Islamic Messianism*:

Mushaf Fatima is described as a scroll three time the size of the Qur'án. The circumstances of its compilation are recounted by Ja'far al-Sadiq (the sixth Imám). He relates that when Fatima was in great sorrow after the death of her father, the Prophet, God sent an angel to console her. She heard the angel's voice speaking to her. She once complained to 'Alí about this strange event, and he asked her to inform him whenever she heard the voice. She did so and he wrote down everything the angel told her. The Mushaf does not say anything about what is lawful and what is unlawful but relates future events. Comparing it to the

Qur'án, the Imám says it contains nothing which was in the Qur'an. It also contains the last will of Fatima and is accompanied by the weapons of the Prophet. Another feature of the Mushaf is that it contains the names of all those who would rule the world, together with their fathers' names.[103]

It was accepted on faith by Shí'í Muslims that the Hidden Book of Fátimih was given to her by the Archangel Gabriel but apart from the Twelve Imams who were supposed to have a copy of it, it was never seen by mortal men. We can, therefore, assume that it has never existed.

Despite its obvious kinship with Arabic literary traditions, the Hidden Words does not have a literary counterpart in Arabo-Persian literature. Bahá'u'lláh has created a unique literary form with the Hidden Words. E. G. Browne, the famed Orientalist, in a footnote to his translation of 'Abdu'l-Bahá's *A Traveller's Narrative*, states that his own search for such a work was fruitless. Browne appends his comment to a line in which 'Abdu'l-Bahá addresses the Shah of Persia:

> A translation of some passages from the contents of the *Hidden Book of Fátimih* (upon her be the blessings of God) . . . will [now] be submitted in the Persian language, in order that some things [now] concealed may be revealed before the [Royal] Presence.[104]

'Abdu'l-Bahá calls the work the *Hidden Book of Fátimih* but then goes on in the next sentence to say that it is 'today known as *Hidden Words*'. Thus when the work was written in 1858, it was first known as the Hidden Book of Fátimih but by 1886, when 'Abdu'l-Bahá wrote *A Traveller's Narrative*, it was known as the Hidden Words. Browne pursued the idea that the book was 'hidden', as well as the belief that it was 'Fátimih's Book' in his efforts to trace back its literary history. The following footnote, though lengthy, illustrates Browne's attempt to find a literary precursor to Bahá'u'lláh's work:

I was at first doubtful as to whether the passages here cited were really translated by Behá from some Arabic work bearing this name, or whether they were in truth extracts from a work of his own called 'Hidden Words' . . . whereof I had heard frequent mention amongst the Bábís. The following passage on p. 379 of Mr Merrick's translation of a work on Shi'ite theology . . . seemed to bear on the question: – 'After the Prophet's death Fáṭima was affected in spirit to a degree which none but God knew. Jebrá'íl was sent down daily to comfort her, and Ali wrote what the angel said, and this is the Book of Fáṭima which is now with the Imám Mahdí.' On consulting Rieu's *Catalogue of the Persian MSS in the British Museum*, I found mention (vol. ii, p. 829 b.) of a work . . . composed by Mullá Muḥsin-i-Feyz of Káshán, and described as consisting of 'one hundred sayings of Imáms and Súfís in Arabic, with Persian commentary.' I seized the first opportunity of examining this work, but a search of about two hours through its pages revealed nothing resembling the passages in the text before us. Finally I wrote to Acre, asking, amongst other questions, what might be the true nature of the work here alluded to. The following answer (which is authoritative) was returned: – [Translation] *'Fifth Question.* Concerning the *Hidden Book of Fáṭima* (upon her be the peace of God). The answer is this, that the sect of Persia, that is the Shi'ites, who regard themselves as pure, and the [rest of the] world (we take refuge with God!) as unclean, believe that after His Highness the Seal of the Prophets Muḥammad Her Highness Fáṭima (upon her be the blessings of God) was occupied night and day in weeping, wailing, and lamenting over the fate of her illustrious father. Therefore was Jebrá'íl commanded by the Lord Most Glorious to commune, converse, and associate with Her Highness Fáṭima; and he used to speak words causing consolation and quietude of heart. These words were collected and named *The Book of Fáṭima* . . . And they [i.e. the Shi'ites] believe that this *Book* is with His Highness the Ká'im [i.e. the Imám Mahdí] and shall appear in the days of his appearance. But of this *Book* nought is known save the name, and indeed it is a name without form and a title without reality. And His Highness the Existent [i.e. Bahá'u'lláh] willed to make known the appearance of the Ká'im by intimation and implication; therefore was it mentioned in this manner for a wise reason which he had. And that which is mentioned under the name of *Book* in the Epistle to His Majesty the King [of Persia] (may God assist him) is from the *Hidden Words* . . . which was revealed before the Epistle to His Majesty the King. The *Hidden Words* was revealed in the languages of eloquence (Arabic) and light (Persian) . . . At all events both the Persian and the Arabic thereof were revealed in *this* manifestation.[105]

As stated, Browne examined the compilation of sayings of Imáms and Sufis compiled by Mullá Muḥsin, doubting that Bahá'u'lláh had penned the Hidden Words and thinking, perhaps, He had plagiarized them from some other work. Finally Browne wrote to Acre, that is, to 'Abdu'l-Bahá, Head of the Bahá'í Faith after Bahá'u'lláh's death, who was resident there. Browne received the explanation current among the Shí'ís that the *Book of Fáṭimih* was given to solace Fáṭimih but was lost with the Twelfth Imám. However, 'Abdu'l-Bahá went on to say that 'of this *Book* nought is known save the name, and indeed it is a name without form and a title without reality'. In other words, according to 'Abdu'l-Bahá, no such book had ever existed. This statement coincided with E. G. Browne's own conclusion. 'Abdu'l-Bahá went on to say that Bahá'u'lláh 'willed to make known the appearance of the Ká'im by intimation and implication; therefore was it mentioned in this manner for a wise reason which he had'. We here have an affirmation by 'Abdu'l-Bahá, as mentioned above, that the work was called *The Book of Fáṭimih* so as to make a theological statement and announce that Bahá'u'lláh was the Qá'im. It is clear that Bahá'u'lláh's Hidden Words is laden with theological allusions and implications relating to more than 1,200 years of the Islamic religion and has grown out of a literary tradition which fluoresced as a result of it.

The major point here, however, is that there is no genre in Arabo-Persian literature into which the Hidden Words of Bahá'u'lláh fits. This does not imply that the Hidden Words emerged in a literary vacuum. No literary work is isolated from its literary tradition and all the influences and restraints of its literary system, as has been demonstrated above. However, it appears that the Hidden Words is a unique literary form and one that is most unlikely to be emulated by others or developed further in the Arabo-Persian literary system.

The Prose Style Used by Bahá'u'lláh in the Hidden Words

Prose in early nineteenth century Persia was at a nadir of florid and linguistic acrobatics. A friend of Bahá'u'lláh's father and high member of the Court, Mírzá Abu'l-Qásim Qá'im-maqám (died 1835), is known for his letters which are models of Persian prose style. He greatly simplified the language of his prose and was much admired.[106] Bahá'u'lláh mentions him in one of His Tablets and was surely aware of his literary innovations. To what extent Bahá'u'lláh was influenced by Qá'im-maqám in His own prose writings is not known. Suffice it to say, in the words of E.G. Brown, 'from the point of view of style, both in Persian and Arabic, an immense improvement was effected by Bahá'u'lláh'.[107]

After the high point in Arabic letters and the invasion of Persia by the Mongols, prose degenerated in all areas including theology, philosophy, the sciences, history and biography. For the reader who might wish to examine the Hidden Words in light of the prose current among Persian of Bahá'u'lláh's time, the following is a translation by E. G. Browne of a 'passage from that very useful and by no means very florid history of the early Ṣafawí period the *Aḥsanu't-Tawáríkh* (985/1577-8)' which 'describes the war waged on the blind Sháhrukh Dhu'l-Qadar by Muḥammad Khán Ustájlú in the spring of 914/1508-9':

In the spring, when the Rose-king with pomp and splendour turned his face to attack the tribes of the Basil, and, with thrusts of his thorn-spear, drove in rout from the Rose-garden the hibernal hosts –
A roar [i.e. the spring thunder] arose from the cloud-drums, the army of the basils was stirred;
The cloud contracted its brows, and drew Rustam-bows [rainbows] for the contest;
The flowering branches raised their standards, the basils prepared their cavalry and their hosts;
The cloud in its skirts bore in every direction hail-stones for the head of Afrásiyáb –
Khán Muḥammad Ustájlú encamped in summer quarters at Márdín.

All this could much better be said in one line . . . 'In the spring Khán Muḥammad Ustájlú encamped in summer quarters at Márdín.'[108]

Browne's statement 'All this could much better be said in one line' says it all. Though we might forgive some of these linguistic pyrotechnics in poetry, in history it goes beyond all bounds of current taste. Of course, every age has its own measure of merit in literary activity but such an overdone prose style, which Browne concedes is not even extreme, has little to recommend it. If we look at the two following Hidden Words in translation, the first from the Persian and the second from the Arabic, the prose style is seen to be simple and direct, yet elegant and lovely, a far cry from the passage above:

82. O My Servant!
The best of men are they that earn a livelihood by their calling and spend upon themselves and upon their kindred for the love of God, the Lord of all worlds.

28. O Son of Spirit!
Know thou of a truth: He that biddeth men be just and himself committeth iniquity is not of Me, even though he bear My name.

Both of these Hidden Words are straightforward and simple. There is no ornamentation or embellishment. Bahá'u'lláh wrote the Hidden Words without self-consciousness, freed from over-used and outdated rhetorical devices. In His prose style Bahá'u'lláh harked back to a simplicity and directness not seen in five or six hundred years.

4

Translations of the Hidden Words

Early Translations

There have been more English translations of the Hidden
Words than any other Bahá'í text. This probably reflects its
popularity in the Bahá'í corpus. The various translators who
tried their hand at the Hidden Words surely sought to
improve the existing translations by couching this work in
a more befitting style of English than had been previously
achieved. This undoubtedly accounts for the many retransla-
tions.

The first translator was E. G. Browne, who translated four
of the Persian Hidden Words (Persian 24, 25, 28 and 30)
into English. These were passages quoted by 'Abdu'l-Bahá
in His own book, *A Traveller's Narrative: Written to Illustrate
the Episode of the Báb*, which Browne translated from Persian
into English and had published in England in 1891. Thus,
the first translator of some of the Hidden Words was a highly
regarded English scholar.

The next translation was made in America by Ibrahim
Kheiralla, a Syrian immigrant to America who gave American
Bahá'ís the first English language text of the Arabic Hidden
Words. Kheiralla's efforts also gave the Bahá'í Faith its first
converts in the United States in 1894. In 1900 he published
his translation of the Arabic Hidden Words as the last chapter of his book *Beha'U'llah*. Kheiralla states at the beginning
of his translation that 'the following utterances, entitled the
"Hidden Words"', are 'literally translated from the Arabic'.
Chart 1 shows Kheiralla's translation of the Prologue and the
first Arabic Hidden Word.

Chart 1

Kheiralla's Translation

1   He is El-behi-ul-abha. This is that which
2   descended from the Majestic Might through the
3   Tongue of Power and Strength upon the prophets
4   of the past. We have taken its essences and
5   clothed them with the garment of Brevity, as a
6   favor upon the divines that they may fulfill the
7   Covenant of God and be able to perform it
8   themselves what He entrusted to them; that they
9   may win, by the essence of piety, in the land
10   of the Spirit, the Victory.
11   O Son of Spirit! The first utterance is,
12   Possess a good, pure and enlightened heart,
13   that thou mayest possess a continual,
14   everlasting, unceasing and ancient Kingdom.[109]

The title page of this 1900 publication shows that Kheiralla's translation was edited by Howard MacNutt, an early American Bahá'í. However, it is safe to say that Kheiralla's English was well grounded. He is assertive and self-confident, expressing the thought, as he understood it, in English that is not slavishly literal, and he is able to change the syntax to achieve a better English style. In contrast to Mrs Jean Stannard, a later translator who put variant meanings of words in parentheses, made annotations and so on, Kheiralla took an unapologetic stand on meaning. Of course, one might argue against this approach for the translation of scripture where error or misinterpretation is considered serious by members of the religion.

Turning to the presentation of the text on the page, Kheiralla includes the invocation 'He is El-behi-ul-abha' (O Thou the Glorious, the Most Glorious – line 1) as part of the opening paragraph. The addresses ('O Son of Being', etc.) appear at the beginning of each Hidden Word as part of the paragraph, and the paragraphs are not numbered or set apart by intervening spaces. It may be that it was Kheiralla who fixed the order of the Hidden Words, followed by every translator after him, since, as noted above, 'the Hidden Words have no sequence'.[110]

In 1905 Dr Ameen U. Fareed's translation of both the Arabic and Persian Hidden Words was published under the title of *Hidden Words, Words of Wisdom and Communes: From 'the Supreme Pen' of Baha'u'llah* by the Bahai Publishing Society in Chicago. Fareed was the nephew of 'Abdu'l-Bahá's wife and 'Abdu'l-Bahá had financed his study of medicine in the United States. Fareed, himself a Persian, was the first to translate the complete Persian Hidden Words into English. He also retranslated the Arabic Hidden Words. Chart 2 gives Fareed's translation of the Prologue and first two Arabic Hidden Words. Note the beginning of Fareed's translation.

Chart 2

Fareed's Translation

1   He is El-Baha-El-Abha!

2   HE IS THE GLORY OF
3   THE MOST GLORIOUS!
4   (1) This is that which descended from the
5   Source of Majesty, through the tongue of Power
6   and Strength upon the prophets of the past. We
7   have taken its essences and clothed them with
8   the garment of brevity, as a favor to the
9   beloved, that they may fulfil the Covenant of
10   God; that they may perform in themselves that
11   which He has entrusted to them, and attain the
12   victory by virtue of devotion in the land of the
13   Spirit:

14   (2) O Son of Spirit!
15   The first counsel is: Possess a good, a
16   pure, an enlightened heart, that thou mayest
17   possess a Kingdom eternal, immortal, ancient,
18   and without end.

Fareed, like Kheiralla, makes definite choices without including distracting notes or alternative words. As to the presentation of the text on the page, Fareed made some innovations over Kheiralla's translation. The invocation, 'He is El-Baha-El-Abha!' (line 1), is not only transliterated (writing or spelling in corresponding characters of another alphabet) differently, and less correctly, but it is set apart from the Prologue and is also translated for the reader: 'HE IS THE GLORY OF THE MOST GLORIOUS!' (lines 2–3). Additionally, each meditation is numbered in parentheses. The addresses, such as 'O Son of Spirit' (line 14), are set on the line above the text of each meditation. Further, each meditation is separated from the preceding by a space. The effect is more pleasing to the eye and greatly simplifies the process of finding a particular passage.

Mrs Jean Stannard, a prominent Bahá'í teacher and traveller from England, published her translation of the Arabic and Persian Hidden Words in Cairo in 1921. Stannard's expertise in Arabic and Persian is not known but she was the first native English speaker to undertake the translation of the full Arabic and Persian texts, Browne having only translated four of the Persian Hidden Words. Chart 3 shows the first page of Stannard's translation of the Arabic Hidden Words.

Chart 3

Stannard's Translation

1   HE IS EL-BAHIO-EL-ABHA!

2   He is The Glory of
3   The Most Glorious !

―――――

4   This is that which was revealed through the
5   tongue of Power and Might upon the Prophets of
6   the past; from the Source of the Most High.*
7   We have taken of its essence and clothed it
8   with the garment of brevity for the sake of the
9   discerning (or perceptive) ones, that they may
10   fulfil in themselves the Covenant of God; and
11   deliver that trust which He hath committed to
12   them; whereby they may be found winners of the
13   jewels of virtue in the realm of Spirit.

14   I. O SON OF SPIRIT.

15   The first of Counsels is this, possess a
16   good, pure and shining (enlightened) heart that
17   thou mayest possess an everlasting, ancient and
18   eternal Kingdom.

―――――

19   * Ar. 'Gaberout'. (of Sublimity). This term
20   frequently used implies might, power,
21   sovereignty, of divine order.

Comparing Stannard's translation with Fareed's, we see quite a number of differences. Stannard has kept the invocation with its translation set apart at the top of the page but uses a different transliteration system, that is, to the extent that any of the translators thus far could be said to have had a system. Transliteration of Bahá'í works, which Shoghi Effendi later standardized according to the usage of scholars of his time, was, at best, haphazard. In addition, Stannard changes the numbering of the Hidden Words, dividing the Prologue into two introductory paragraphs, and beginning number one of the first meditation with an address, here 'O Son of Spirit!' (line 14). Her approach to the text is also quite different. She is obviously in awe of the 'Word of God', as she perceives it, and is much more cautious in her approach. This we infer from her generous use of parenthetical alternative readings. Also, her text has footnotes to amplify her translation. A remark, presumably hers, in the Preface indicates that 'during the work of collaboration it became evident that certain footnotes and explanatory comments were indispensable for elucidating some of the intricate symbolic terms and phrases'. To supplement the numerous parenthetical inclusions and the annotations, there is a four-page appendix at the end of the book giving additional information about the significance of certain passages of the Hidden Words which Stannard gathered from 'Abdu'l-Bahá while on her visits to the Holy Land. Furthermore, Stannard includes the complete Arabic and Persian texts for those who can read the originals. Certainly her effort produces the most comprehensive volume of the Hidden Words with a sincere attempt to include scholarly notes to allow the reader more access to the text. Of course, serious scholarly commentary on the Hidden Words would be a lengthy undertaking, resulting in a sizeable volume. Unfortunately, contrary to Stannard's intentions, the alternative readings and notes are distracting to the reader who wishes a straightforward approach to the heart of the work and often merely raise more questions than they answer. To what extent this volume gained currency in the United States, where most of the Bahá'í works in English were published, is not known. However, only two years later, in 1923, Shoghi Effendi, by then Guardian of the Bahá'í Faith, translated the Hidden Words and the focus since that time has been on his rendition of the work, to which we will now turn.

An Overview of Shoghi Effendi's Translation of the Hidden Words into English, and Revisions

Shoghi Effendi became Guardian of the Bahá'í Faith in January 1922 when the Will of 'Abdu'l-Bahá appointing him to that office was read. From that time until his death in November 1957 he did all the official translations of Bahá'í texts from the original Arabic and Persian into English. The first translation he made after assuming the Guardianship was of the Will and Testament of 'Abdu'l-Bahá into English. His next translation was the Hidden Words, both Arabic and Persian. He was not new to translation since his education had been designed in part to enable him to assist 'Abdu'l-Bahá by translating His Tablets into English. Shoghi Effendi had worked as 'Abdu'l-Bahá's secretary for two years before studying at Oxford. He also translated Bahá'í texts while at Oxford.

The earliest known translation of the Hidden Words by Shoghi Effendi is that published by the Bahai Assembly at London in 1923 under the cover title of *Hidden Words, Words of Wisdom, Prayers*.[111] This was reprinted in New York by the Baha'i Publishing Committee in 1924 and again in 1925. The 1924 edition contain eight pages of other material by Bahá'u'lláh, including a translation of 'Words of Wisdom'. The 1925 edition contains a revised Foreword in which Shoghi Effendi mentions the Stannard translation. Thus from at least 1925 onwards we can say with certainty that Shoghi Effendi was familiar with Mrs Stannard's translation of the Hidden Words.

In 1929 the National Spiritual Assembly of the Bahá'ís of

Great Britain and Northern Ireland published in London *The Hidden Words of Bahá'u'lláh*, a revised translation of the work. On the title page is the following: 'Translated by Shoghi Effendi with the assistance of some English friends.' These English friends were George Townshend and Ethel Rosenberg, about which more will be said later. Of note here is that Shoghi Effendi sought out able English speakers to help him.

The text of the 1929 translation was reprinted by the National Spiritual Assembly of the Bahá'ís of the British Isles in 1932 and by the Bahá'í Publishing Committee at New York in the same year. Since then the 1929 translation has been reprinted many times in both the United States and the United Kingdom. Some words are spelled differently in the 1940 edition printed in the United States but these are limited to Americanization of English spelling, probably to adapt the text to American readers. For example, Hidden Word Arabic 2 in the 1929 British edition has the words 'neighbour' and 'behoveth'; these are spelled 'neighbor' and 'behooveth' in the 1932 edition reprinted in the United States in 1940. However, it is the same translation and not a revision.

The next revision took place in 1954 during the Guardianship of Shoghi Effendi. The copyright page of the 1963 edition of the Hidden Words published in the United States gives the copyright as 1954 by the National Spiritual Assembly of the Bahá'ís of the United States, revised edition. Shoghi Effendi himself would have revised the translation since he did not die until 1957.

Translation or Revision?

We now turn to a consideration of the 1923 edition of the Hidden Words of Bahá'u'lláh, which was probably Shoghi Effendi's original translation of the work. The first question we might ask is, did he revise an earlier translation or did he do his own? At what point does revision of someone else's work become a new work, worthy of being considered a new translation in its own right? There is no hard and fast rule by which to determine the answer to such a question. The answer must necessarily be subjective to some degree. However, it should be possible to establish a consensus. We shall proceed with the assumption that a plausible resolution is in the realm of possibility.

To begin to answer the question, the translations of Fareed, Stannard and Shoghi Effendi of the Prologue and the first 20 Arabic Hidden Words were compared side by side (see Table 1; since Kheiralla made the first translation into English of the Arabic Hidden Words, his translation is not included). Fareed had only Kheiralla's text to work with, so any passages he revised were of necessity those of Kheiralla. Three categories were created to account for the tenor of the individual passage. A revision (r) means that there is minimal change, perhaps the correction of an error in meaning or stating something more succinctly or felicitously. A translation (t) indicates that the text is obviously a new rendition with little or no influence from earlier versions. In between these two categories a classification (r-t) was created to cover those passages that were neither revisions nor translations in their own right. In these there is some revision but also some degree of originality. If there is any argument as to designation, it would be in this grey area. Frequent reference has been made to the Arabic original, for often the original text itself binds the translator and produces a similarity in phrasing among translators. In such cases, even if the translator had come to the source work fresh, having looked at no other translations, he would most probably have chosen the same words or phrases as earlier translators. In these instances the translator was given the benefit of the doubt and his predictable word choice was not considered to have been influenced by earlier translations.

Let us now look at the results of an analysis of 21 of the 72 passages of the Arabic Hidden Words, nearly a third of the entire work. (For the text of these passages see Appendix 3).

This should be quite adequate to determine any patterns in this work as a whole.

As can be seen from Table 1, clear patterns emerge in the cases of Stannard and Shoghi Effendi. Stannard has obviously revised Fareed's work while Shoghi Effendi has translated the Hidden Words and not revised it.

Fareed, interestingly enough, has approximately seven passages in each category (8 in r, 6 in t, 7 in r-t). His work is sufficiently different from Kheiralla's work not to be called a revision, although a substantial number of Hidden Words are revised. However, nearly an equal number are new translations of passages. His work seems to straddle the line between revision and translation but is neither. Since it seems to be something else, let us call it a 'translation-revision'. It is obvious that Fareed worked closely with Kheiralla's text and he must be credited with taking the 'rough' translation of Kheiralla and 'cleaning it up' considerably. Of course, just as Kheiralla made the first translation of the Arabic Hidden Words into English, Fareed did the first translation of the complete Persian Hidden Words into English, which in the 1905 publication gave English readers the complete work in English for the first time.

Stannard's revision of Fareed's text is puzzling. She must have been dissatisfied with Fareed's translation, otherwise why would she translate it anew? Her translation is so closely based on Fareed's translation that it must be called a revision, although some passages are noticeably different. Stannard makes 16 revisions of Fareed's text, only one of them also revising Kheiralla's rendition. Five of the passages are revision-translations. Clearly, she has revised Fareed's work and cannot be said to have done a translation in the sense of original work. In most passages she uses Fareed's phrasing with only a word or two changed. The prose, which she obviously sought to improve over Fareed's rendition, though well-intentioned, is not more noteworthy. In a few instances her wording is much lovelier but, surprisingly, for the most part, there is no improvement or there is an actual

Table 1

Hidden Words	Fareed	Stannard	Shoghi Effendi
Prologue	r	r-t(F)	t
1	r-t	r-t(F)	t
2	r-t	r-t(F)(Kh)	t
3	t	r(F)	t
4	r	r(F)	t
5	r	r(F)	r(F)
6	r-t	r-t(F)	t
7	t	r(F)	r-t(F)
8	t	r(F)	t
9	r	r(F)	t
10	r-t	r(F)	t
11	r	r(F)	t
12	r	r(F)	t
13	r	r(F)	t
14	r-t	r(F)	t
15	t	r-t(F)	t
16	r	r(F)	t
17	t	r(F)	t
18	r-t	r(F)	t
19	r-t	r(F)	t
20	t	r(F)	t

The first column gives the passage being examined. The following three columns show the translations of Fareed and Stannard and the 1923 translation of Shoghi Effendi. If a passage is considered a revision, the initial of the translator whose work is being revised is indicated in parentheses.

deterioration of quality. This is not surprising as her translation is pedantic. Some of these reversals include stretching normal English syntax and having run-on sentences without punctuation. Her parenthetical inclusions and footnotes also diminish the work. On the other hand, her inclusion of additional information with an Appendix, original Arabic and Persian texts and a brief Tablet from 'Abdu'l-Bahá commending her effort should be noted.

Table 1 shows that Shoghi Effendi's case is the clearest with 19 out of 21 passages being translations and not revisions. He did revise one passage of Fareed's, Arabic 6; and Arabic 7 is a revision-translation, also of Fareed's text. Since Fareed's work was a major improvement over Kheiralla's effort, it is possible that Shoghi Effendi had only a cursory acquaintance with Kheiralla's translation.

Shoghi Effendi was surely very familiar with Fareed's translation of the Hidden Words. His familiarity with it must have begun at the very least during his year and a half in Oxford; English Bahá'ís would have been using Fareed's translation since its publication in 1905. Further, English-speaking pilgrims had been coming to Acre since Shoghi Effendi was three or four years old and, as we have seen, English was already a feature of 'Abdu'l-Bahá's household in 1905, when Shoghi Effendi was about eight years old. Western pilgrims no doubt brought with them the English translation of the Hidden Words. It is possible that 'Abdu'l-Bahá had the young Shoghi Effendi read the English translations of Bahá'u'lláh's works as part of his education in the language. Thus Shoghi Effendi was probably quite familiar with Fareed's translation of the Hidden Words yet he was still able to distance himself from it enough to translate the work and not revise it. It is perhaps surprising that he was able to do so and indicates that he was not bound by one way of looking at the text.

Here is Shoghi Effendi's 1923 translation of the first page of the Hidden Words:

Chart 4

Shoghi Effendi's Translation

1   He is the Glory of Glories

2   This is that which hath descended from the
3   Realm of Glory, uttered by the Tongue of Power
4   and Might and revealed unto the Messengers of
5   old, the quintessence whereof We have taken and
6   arrayed in the garment of brevity, as a token of
7   grace unto the righteous that they may stand
8   faithful unto the Covenant of the Lord, that
9   they may fulfill in their lives His Trust, and
10   may in the Realm of the Spirit obtain for
11   themselves the priceless gem of Divine Virtue.

12   (1) O SON OF SPIRIT!
13   My first counsel is this: Possess a pure,
14   kindly and radiant heart, that thine may be a
15   sovereignty, heavenly, ancient, imperishable
16   and everlasting.

This passage consists of the Prologue and the first Hidden Word of the Arabic. Let us now examine Shoghi Effendi's translation of part of this page against the work of earlier translators to illustrate how it can be said that Shoghi Effendi's is a new translation and not a revision. Following are the opening lines of the text by Kheiralla, Fareed, Stannard and Shoghi Effendi, respectively:

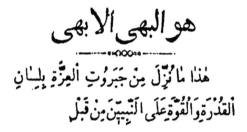

Kheiralla:

1 He is El-behi-ul-abha. This is that which
2 descended from the Majestic Might through the
3 Tongue of Power and Strength upon the prophets
4 of the past.

Fareed:

HE IS EL-BAHA-EL-ABHA!

*He Is The Glory of
The Most Glorious!*

4 (1) This is that which descended from the
5 Source of Majesty, through the tongue of Power
6 and Strength upon the prophets of the past.

Stannard:

HE IS EL-BAHIO-EL-ABHA!

He is The Glory of
The Most Glorious!

4   This is that which was revealed through the
5   tongue of Power and Might upon the Prophets of
6   the past; from the Source of the Most High.

Shoghi Effendi:

He is the Glory of Glories.

2   This is that which hath descended from the
3   Realm of Glory, uttered by the Tongue of Power
4   and Might and revealed unto the Messengers of
5   old . . .

Let us begin with the choice of the word 'glory' for the invocation. The Arabic هو البهى الابهى refers to God and also to Bahá'u'lláh as God's messenger. The word بهاء (bahá') in Arabic and Persian primarily means 'beauty' but has several related meanings: 'splendour; effulgence; glory'. The Báb gave Bahá'u'lláh His title meaning 'Glory of God'. Bahá'u-'lláh Himself emphasized the concept of glory associated with His name. In one Tablet, for example, while alluding to Himself, He quotes the Arabic text of Isaiah 2:10 which in the King James version reads: 'Enter into the rock, and hide thee in the dust for fear of the Lord and for the glory of his majesty.' The Arabic reads:

ادخل الى الصخرة و اختبى فى التراب من امام هيبة الرب و
من بهاء عظمتة [112]

From the earliest time, Bahá'ís attached the concept of glory, as reflected in splendour or effulgence, to Bahá'u'lláh's name. Although 'beauty' is the primary meaning of the term ﺑﻬﺎﺀ (bahá'), yet as associated with His name, the peripheral connotation of 'glory' has always been uppermost among Bahá'ís. This might explain why Fareed, who first translated the invocation, used 'glory' and not 'beauty' in 'He is the Glory of the Most Glorious!' Each subsequent translator followed Fareed's choice of the word 'glory', including Shoghi Effendi.

The invocation shows a marked development in the hands of each translator. Kheiralla chose to translate 'He is' and simply transliterated the remainder: 'He is El-behi-ul-abha.' Fareed went a step further and translated it into English after citing the transliteration, which is somewhat different from Kheiralla's transliteration: 'HE IS EL-BAHA EL-ABHA! He is the Glory of The Most Glorious!' Thus Fareed kept the 'He is' with the Arabic, as did Kheiralla, but he transliterated 'El-behi' as 'El-Baha,' which is grammatically incorrect. He then repeats 'He is' in the translation 'He is the Glory of The Most Glorious'. Fareed seems to have interpreted this as a posses-sive, 'The Glory of the Most Glorious'. Stannard kept Fareed's rendition, except that she corrected his 'El-Baha' to 'El-Bahio'. Felicitously, Shoghi Effendi eliminated the clumsy and distracting transliteration and simplified the invocation to 'He is the Glory of Glories'.

Fareed was the first to translate the invocation, Stannard revised one letter only and Shoghi Effendi changed it suffi-ciently to be in the category of revision-translation. We shall later examine the invocation and Prologue as a whole to determine their status.

Each translator opens the Prologue with the words 'This is that which', as first rendered by Kheiralla. They might have chosen 'This is what' instead but perhaps they consid-ered this alternative less lovely and dignified. Whatever the reason, this phrase was not retranslated by any of them.

Fareed removes the invocation from the body of the text, where Kheiralla originally put it, but uses the same verb – 'descended' – in the opening phrase: 'This is that which descended'. Stannard keeps the phrase 'This is that which' used by both Kheiralla and Fareed but uses the verb 're-vealed' instead of 'descended'. Shoghi Effendi goes back to the verb 'descended' but changes the tense to 'hath de-scended'.

Fareed keeps Kheiralla's phrase 'through the Tongue of Power and Strength'. Stannard changes it to 'through the tongue of Power and Might'. Shoghi Effendi keeps her modification – 'the Tongue of Power and Might' – while capitalizing 'Might', but adds the verbal phrase 'uttered by'. Thus, the two phrases Shoghi Effendi retains from the Stannard translation are 'This is that which' and 'Power and Might'.

The word 'tongue' لسان in the phrase 'tongue of power and might', is bound by the text in that there is no other word to use in English unless one chooses to move away into an interpretative rendition and use 'language' as in 'in the language of Power and Might'. However, this would alter the meaning since 'tongue of power and might' suggests that God's Being is speaking, that is, the actor is performing an action, whereas 'language' is the product of the actor's action. By capitalizing 'Tongue' Shoghi Effendi emphasizes that the Deity is speaking. 'Tongue', then, functions in the text as synecdoche. To substitute the word 'language' would alter the meaning. For this reason 'tongue' is considered to be bound by the text.

Fareed keeps the phrase 'upon the prophets of the past' which Kheiralla originally used, and Stannard also retains it although she capitalizes 'Prophet'. Shoghi Effendi trans-lates this as 'revealed unto the Messengers of old'. Shoghi Effendi here departs from the 'prophet' used by previous translators, which is the usual translation of نبی (nabí), and interprets it as 'Messengers'. In Arabic there is a distinction between prophets نبیین (nabiyín) and messengers رسل (rusul). 'Prophets' generally refers to the major and minor prophets of the Old Testament and the like, whereas 'mes-sengers' is reserved for such initiators of religions as Moses,

Christ and Muḥammad. Obviously Shoghi Effendi interprets this passage differently from the previous translators. Further, he has moved sufficiently far from the earlier renditions to be translating this phrase and not revising it.

The words 'descended' and 'revealed' are used in the earlier renditions, as they are the best choices to impart the meaning of the Arabic نزل (nazala) which has the sense of a divine book being sent down by God. This is the verb used to describe the revelation of the Qur'án, it having been sent down to Muḥammad to reveal to man. Shoghi Effendi could have used 'sent down', 'come down' or 'given to' but kept 'descended' and 'revealed', which are better choices.

If we look again at these lines translated by Shoghi Effendi, this time putting in parentheses the words that are bound to the original text and which could hardly have been put otherwise, and italicizing the words he retained from earlier translations, we have the following:

2   *This is that which* hath *descended* from the
3   Realm of Glory, uttered by the (Tongue) of *Power*
4   *and Might* and revealed unto the Messengers of
5   old . . .

Most of this passage, then, is new. Since we are excluding the word in parentheses, the only material Shoghi Effendi uses in common with earlier translators is 'This is that which,' 'descended' and 'Power and Might.' For this reason, Shoghi Effendi's version is considered to be a translation and not a revision.

Let us now look at the next lines of the Prologue:

وَإِنَّا أَخَذْنَا
جَوَاهِرَهُ وَأَقْمَصْنَاهُ قَمِيصَ الِاخْتِصَارِ فَضْلًا
عَلَى الْأَحْبَارِ لِيُوفُوا بِعَهْدِ اللَّهِ

Kheiralla:

4   We have taken its essences and
5   clothed them with the garment of Brevity, as a
6   favor upon the divines that they may fulfill the
7   Covenant of God

Fareed:

6   We
7   have taken its essences and clothed them with
8   the garment of brevity, as a favor to the
9   beloved, that they may fulfil the Covenant of
10   God;

Stannard:

7   We have taken of its essence and clothed it
8   with the garment of brevity for the sake of the
9   discerning (or perceptive) ones, that they may
10   fulfil in themselves the Covenant of God;

Shoghi Effendi:

5   the quintessence whereof We have taken and
6   arrayed in the garment of brevity, as a token of
7   grace unto the righteous that they may stand
8   faithful unto the Covenant of the Lord,

Fareed keeps Kheiralla's exact rendition here with the exception of one phrase: he changes the reading of Kheiralla's 'as a favor upon the divines' to 'as a favor to the beloved'. The original Arabic word is الاحبار (al-ahbár) , the plural of 'a non-Muslim religious authority, learned man, scribe; bishop; rabbi'. Kheiralla uses the word 'divines' to encompass the sense of 'clergy' whereas Fareed uses 'beloved' which is simply a misreading of احبار as احباب, an easy mistake especially from a written manuscript. Stannard also keeps most of these lines, changing 'its essences' to 'of its essence', which then required her to use 'clothed it' instead of 'clothed them'. However, she uses the less lovely 'for the sake of the discerning (or perceptive) ones' for Kheiralla's 'as a favor upon the divines' or Fareed's 'as a favor to the beloved'. Furthermore, Stannard sacrifices loveliness altogether in an attempt to be literal. Her desire for precision is jarring, particularly the parenthetical intrusion.

Finally, Fareed keeps Kheiralla's 'that they may fulfill the Covenant of God'. Stannard adds 'in themselves' to this phrase. Shoghi Effendi changes it altogether to 'that they may stand faithful unto the Covenant of the Lord'. It is interesting to observe here that although Shoghi Effendi has in this version moved away from 'the Covenant of God' used by earlier translators, in his 1925 revision he goes back to it. In order to remain faithful to the original بعهد الله , he could only reasonably choose between 'the Covenant of the Lord' or 'the Covenant of God'. Thus, this phrase, too, is limited by the original.

If we look at this section as we did the previous one, we find the following:

5   the quintessence whereof *We have taken* and
6   arrayed in the *garment of brevity*, as a token of
7   grace unto the righteous (that they may) stand
8   faithful unto the (Covenant) of the Lord,

Shoghi Effendi retains only 'We have taken' and 'garment of brevity' from the earlier renditions. He uses the phrase 'We have taken' although he could have used another. He might have chosen another word for 'garment' قميص, which is a tunic, although it is doubtful that 'garment' can be improved upon, which is probably why he did not retranslate it. However, the Arabic word اخذ has the first dictionary meaning of 'to take'. The phrase in parentheses – 'that they may' – is dictated by the verb tense and remains constant. Most of this section, then, is also new and, therefore, considered translation and not revision.

Let us now consider Hidden Word Arabic 19 to illustrate that Shoghi Effendi's rendition is a translation:

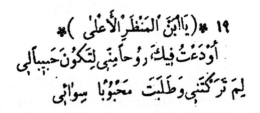

Kheiralla:

1   O Son of the Highest Appearance! I deposited
2   in thee a Spirit from Me that thou might'st be
3   My Lover: Why hast thou left Me and sought
4   another lover?

Fareed:

1   (2) O SON OF THE HIGHEST SIGHT!

2   I have placed within thee a spirit from Me,
3   that thou mightest be My Lover: Why has thou
4   forsaken Me and sought to love another?

Stannard:

1   19. O CHILD OF SUPREME VISION.*

2   I have placed within thee a spirit from
3   Myself, that thou mightest become My lover. Why
4   has thou forsaken Me and sought to love
5   another.

Shoghi Effendi:

1   19. O SON OF THE WONDROUS VISION!

2   I have breathed in thee a breath of My spirit,
3   that thou mayest love Me. Why has thou forsaken
4   Me and sought a beloved other than Me?

Each translator renders the address differently. The words
'O Son' ابن يا are bound by the Arabic text. In English there
is no other translation for the Arabic vocative particle يا
except 'O', which is used by every translator. Of course, it
could be eliminated, but that would remove the intimacy of
being directly addressed and would corrupt the original
meaning. In Stannard's rendition, 'child' strays from the
source text, which says 'son'. There are possibilities such as
'man child', or 'male offspring', but such choices would
diminish the work and also alter the meaning, which collec-
tively addresses both male and female. Shoghi Effendi,
however, has retained Stannard's word 'vision'. Each translator, including Shoghi Effendi, has used 'spirit'. Shoghi
Effendi has also retained the phrase, originally from Fareed,
'Why hast thou forsaken Me and sought'.

The words 'love' and 'beloved' are tied to the primary
dictionary meaning of the Arabic حب (hubb). Shoghi Effendi
uses the term 'wondrous' for الاعلى, which has a first dictionary meaning of 'Highest' or 'Most Exalted' and which he

89

may have chosen in order to give some parameters to a mystical term which cannot be adequately translated.

The original phrases in Shoghi Effendi's rendition are 'wondrous', 'I have breathed in thee a breath of My', 'that thou mayest love Me' and 'a beloved other than Me'. If we look at his translation of this Hidden Word as we did the two previous passages, we have the following:

1   19. (O Son) of the Wondrous *Vision!*

2   I have breathed in thee a breath of My *spirit,*
3   that thou mayest (love) Me. *Why has thou forsaken*
4   *Me and sought* a beloved other than Me?

Shoghi Effendi has kept parts of the earlier renditions in 'vision', 'spirit', and 'Why hast thou forsaken Me and sought'. Some of the passage is source-oriented and the words 'O Son' and 'love' cannot be rendered otherwise without moving away from the meaning. If these words and phrases are excluded, enough original material has been presented to classify this Hidden Word as a translation.

Fareed and Stannard each revised the work that preceded them. Shoghi Effendi obviously closely examined the earlier translations. However, even in his earliest translation he moves away from earlier renditions made by other translators. It should be added that Shoghi Effendi's 1923 rendering was made by a young man and is an example of his earliest efforts. Shoghi Effendi's main revision of 1929 is conspicuously different from the 1923 version, is highly refined and moves a good deal farther away from his first translation.

Shoghi Effendi revised the 1923 translation several times. When referring to those changed texts, the word 'revision' will be used and not 'translation', which refers here to his initial rendering only.

The English Style Used by Shoghi Effendi in His Translation of the Hidden Words

The style Shoghi Effendi used for his translation of the Hidden Words and all his subsequent revisions and translations can best be described as Victorian. Such a style was already dated and conservative at the time Shoghi Effendi first began to work on the Hidden Words. As Guardian of the Bahá'í Faith, he could have chosen another literary style altogether in which to render this work and his other translations as well. He was free to choose any English style he wished or saw fit. Indeed, he could have chosen to translate the Bahá'í writings into another language instead of English, and, in fact, he did consider French as the possible medium for all of his translations.[113] However, it was English of a Victorian tone in the general literary style used for all earlier English translations of the Hidden Words that Shoghi Effendi used. Browne was the first translator to render some of the Bahá'í writings into English, including four of the Persian Hidden Words. Chronologically a Victorian himself, Browne set the Victorian style which the subsequent translators of the Hidden Words – Kheiralla, Fareed, Stannard and Shoghi Effendi – followed.

We should define what we mean by the 'Victorian style'. By this is meant the diction and prosody developed and popularized by such poets as Lord Tennyson and Matthew Arnold and employed also by contemporary translators who worked with Middle Eastern literature. Although, of course, each writer has his own individual mark, this type of literature is distinguished by a very poetic diction not normally used for speech. Indeed, when the expression 'poetic diction' is used, it is often to specify Victorian poetry in particular. In other words, one language is for poetry and another for discourse. Of course, this is true, for the most part, of all literature, but it is more exaggerated in this particular style of English. Furthermore, since the Middle East is exotic, far away and has ancient roots, there is a tendency to use archaicisms and somewhat biblical language to evoke in the reader associations with life in the days of the Patriarchs or the courts of the Sultans.

Browne, in his book *A Year Amongst the Persians*, recounts his experience and adventures during his year in Persia. He is a skilful writer and at times uses very formal and eloquent language which is highly stylized, especially for his translations of old Arabic sayings, such as the following:

> And he who hopes to scale the heights with
>   enduring pain,
> And toil and strife, but wastes his life in idle
>   quest and vain.[114]

Browne's tone here is close to that used in his translation of the four Persian Hidden Words, two of which follow:

> O child of the world! Many a morning hath the effulgence of my grace come unto thy place from the day-spring of the place-less, found thee on the couch of ease busied with other things, and returned like the lightning of the spirit to the bright abode of glory. And I, desiring not thy shame, declared it not in the retreats of nearness to the hosts of holiness.
>
> So likewise he saith:–
>
> O pretender to my friendship! In the morning the breeze of my grace passed by thee, and found thee sleeping on the bed of heedlessness, and wept over thy condition, and turned back.'[115]

This passage is clearly at the opposite end of the spectrum from speech and its style is traditionally the most revered form of English. It employs the informal archaic personal and possessive pronouns 'thy' and 'thee' rather than 'you' and 'your'. The archaic form of the auxiliary verb 'has' – 'hath' is used. Both of these features are hallmarks of biblical English. This style has been used in very formal poetry as well. However, Browne did not capitalize the pronouns referring to the deity; this is curious since even mundane texts of the time would most likely do so. In one of the other Hidden Words Browne translated he did capitalize words referring obviously to God but chose not to in this case. In the Hidden Words above it is plain that the Godhead is speaking, as it was in the Sacred Traditions mentioned earlier. Perhaps Browne felt it was Bahá'u'lláh's voice as well and he was fearful that Western readers would interpret such capitalization as being a tacit endorsement of the text's religious merits or those of its author. Even so, ignoring this element, the translation of these two Hidden Words has a biblical tone. Furthermore, that Browne chose such a style for his translations indicates that he considered the Hidden Words to be serious religious literature.

The translators of Middle Eastern literary works and scripture such as the Qur'án who lived during the Victorian period were receptive to the norms for serious literature then current. With the exception of FitzGerald, who may have adapted a foreign form and given English poetry a new sound, these translators were followers and not innovators. Let us now look at some examples of writers of this period.

The famous tales of the Thousand and One Nights have been translated several times. Of particular interest here are the translations by Andrew Lang and Edward Burton. Edward Burton's translation of several volumes, *The Book of the Thousand Nights and a Night*, 1885, exhibits a very affected and ornamented prose style in keeping with the norms for translated Oriental literature. Following is a brief excerpt for examination:

> But when it was midnight Shahrazad awoke and signalled to her sister Dunyazad who sat up and said, 'Allah upon thee, O my sister, recite to us some new story, delightsome and delectable, wherewith to while away the waking hours of our latter night.' 'With joy and goodly gree,' answered Shahrazad, 'if this pious and auspicious King permit me.' 'Tell on,' quoth the King who chanced to be sleepless and

restless and therefore was pleased with the prospect of hearing her story.[116]

Burton has intentionally tried in his translation to keep as much of the structure and rhyme of the original as possible. He has kept the Arabic *saj'*, or rhymed prose, wherever he could or replaced it with alliteration. For example, 'goodly gree' and 'permit me' are obvious attempts to recreate the *saj'* of the original. There is purposeful rhyme, such as 'midnight', 'recite', 'delightsome' and 'night'. Alliteration appears as 'delightsome' and 'delectable' and 'wherewith', 'while' and 'waking'. Burton uses several archaic words: 'thee', 'goodly gree' and 'quoth'. This passage is far removed from anything approximating speech. It is an embellished style purposely intended to create a period atmosphere and recreate the original as closely as possible. It now sounds quaint, even silly. However, Burton's style varies in his translation, depending on the story and whether it is dialogue or narrative. The above is an example of his more ornamented writing.

Lang's translation of *The Arabian Nights Entertainments*, 1898, is edited and abridged and was created for children. He translated it from the French translation of Monsieur Galland. Let us look at a passage:

> In the times of the Caliph Haroun-al-Rachin there lived in Bagdad a poor porter named Hindbad, who on a very hot day was sent to carry a heavy load from one end of the city to the other. Before he had accomplished half the distance he was so tired that, finding himself in a quiet street where the pavement was sprinkled with rose water, and a cool breeze was blowing, he set his burden upon the ground, and sat down to rest in the shade of a grand house. Very soon he decided that he could not have chosen a pleasanter place; a delicious perfume of aloes wood and pastilles came from the open windows and mingled with the scent of the rose water which steamed up from the hot pavement. Within the palace he heard some music, as of many instru-

ments cunningly played, and the melodious warble of
nightingales and other birds, and by this, and the appetiz-
ing smell of many dainty dishes of which he presently
became aware, he judged that feasting and merry-making
were going on.[117]

Lang's rendition of the tales of the Thousand and One
Nights is not contrived like Burton's translation. Lang, like
the other Victorians, tries to create beauty in his writing.
Here it is beauty leading to wonderment – the wonder of
fairy-tales directed to children. In this passage he uses words
as lovely as possible to describe sensory sensations: 'the
delicious perfume of aloes wood and pastilles' mingling 'with
the scent of rose water' steaming up 'from the hot pavement'
and the smell of 'dainty dishes of which he presently became
aware'. The aural sense is also engaged by 'some music, as
of many instruments cunningly played, and the melodious
warble of nightingales and other birds'. It is apparent that
Lang is intentionally trying to create a rare and beautiful
moment by carefully choosing his words. Although this
passage is far more straightforward than Burton's, Lang also
uses alliteration such as 'pleasanter place', 'perfume', 'pastilles' and 'pavement' all in one sentence. Another example
is 'dainty dishes' and 'merry-making'. Lang's style is more
subtle and more lovely.

Let us now turn away from prose to Victorian poetry.
Matthew Arnold's poem *Sohrab and Rustum* is set in Persia.
Consider this moment of grief:

So, on the bloody sand, Sohrab lay dead;
And the great Rustum drew his horseman's cloak
Down o'er his face, and sate by his dead son.
As those black granite pillars, once high-reared
By Jemshid in Persepolis, to bear
His house, now 'mid their broken flights of steps
Lie prone, enormous, down the mountain side –
So in the sand lay Rustum by his son.[118]

This poem deals with lofty themes and universal questions, as do the tales of the Thousand and One Nights, but in a very different format. However, there are stylistic similarities. Arnold is striving to elevate his language to fit the theme. He also seeks to write in language as beautiful as possible, by Victorian standards, and this means embellished and eloquent. To these ends he uses, among other things, archaisms, as in the words 'o'er' and 'sate'. His diction is peculiar to poetry and other serious literature of the time and to scripture generally. In this passage, 'high-reared' is an example. The rhythm here is carefully planned with ten syllables to each line. Arnold uses alliteration in the repetition of the initial 's' sound, three times in the first line as in 'so', 'sand' and 'Sohrab'. Of course, this is poetry of which rhythm and alliteration are hallmarks. But the elevated tone, the eloquence and beauty are features of Victorian English.

FitzGerald with his masterly translation of the *Rubáiyát of Omar Khayyám* has recreated a work that stands on its own merits as part of the canon of English literature. Consider the well-known quatrain 11:

> Here with a loaf of bread beneath the bough,
> A flask of wine, a book of verse – and thou
> Beside me singing in the wilderness –
> And wilderness is paradise enow.[119]

The quatrain dictates a highly structured form, which Fitz-Gerald follows, here four lines with final end rhyme on lines 1, 2 and 4. We expect poetry to have rhyme and metre and alliteration, which we see here. Of particular interest is the use of the archaic words 'thou' and 'enow'. FitzGerald, like other translators of Middle Eastern literature of his era, uses archaisms. His tone is elevated and eloquent.

A later translator and respected Orientalist, Reynold A. Nicholson, who was a contemporary of Shoghi Effendi and who died in 1945, followed the Victorians' precedent when he translated selections of poetry from the famous Persian mystic poet Rumi. Consider the following untitled poem, sometimes referred to as 'The Reed':

> Hearken to this Reed forlorn,
> Breathing, even since 'twas torn
> From its rushy bed, a strain
> Of impassioned love and pain.
>
> 'The secret of my song, though near,
> None can see and none can hear.
> Oh, for a friend to know the sign
> And mingle all his soul with mine!
>
> 'Tis the flame of Love that fired me,
> 'Tis the wine of Love inspired me.
> Wouldst thou learn how lovers bleed,
> Hearken, hearken to the Reed!'[120]

This poem has the elevated mystic theme of the lover being torn from his prebirth state of unity with the divine to be thrust unwillingly into this world, all the while yearning to return to the Beloved. This is a highly structured poem both in metre and rhyme. Nicholson, whose poems have been well received, uses archaisms, 'hearken', ''twas', ''tis' and 'forlorn' as have the other translators we have discussed. His style is elevated, befitting the subject matter, and he strives for beauty of expression.

Several elements have been observed as features of Victorian English. Overall, there is an attempt to elevate the tone of the writing, to write eloquently and to create beauty. There is also a formality that results from this elevation, a distancing of the utterance through language artifice which is dignified when successful and mawkish when too contrived, that allows expression of emotions and feelings bordering on sentimentalism. Thus profound emotion is expressed in lofty terms, which by contemporary taste risks sounding maudlin. In the English used for translations of Middle Eastern literature and creative literature about the Arab lands during the Victorian period, we find frequent use of archaisms, alliteration and other poetic devices.

We find all these features of English used by Shoghi Effendi in his translation of the Hidden Words. By way of further illustration, let us examine the following Hidden Word Arabic 44 from the 1954 revision:

44. O SON OF THE THRONE!

Thy hearing is My hearing, hear thou therewith. Thy sight is My sight, do thou see therewith, that in thine inmost soul thou mayest testify unto My exalted sanctity, and I within Myself may bear witness unto an exalted station for thee.

The tone here is elevated and fulfils expectations for scripture. Capitalization for 'My' and 'Myself' indicates that the Deity is speaking. The archaic pronouns 'thou', 'thine' and 'thee' are used. Such phrases as 'inmost soul' and 'exalted sanctity' are employed for the sake of creating associations of grandeur in the text. The tone is necessarily distanced since it is scriptural, with man being addressed as 'O Son of the Throne'. Poetic devices are also used to elevate and beautify the text, such as the alliteration in the repetition of the initial 's' sound in the second sentence: 'sight', 'see', 'soul', 'sanctity' and 'station' and internally in 'inmost', 'mayest', 'testify,' 'Myself' and 'witness'. Additionally there is repetition of 'therewith'. Although Shoghi Effendi has his own voice and individual style of writing, overall he uses Victorian English as the medium for his translation of the Hidden Words.

Shoghi Effendi's Known Literary Taste

Shoghi Effendi's styles are, in fact, accurate reflections of his literary tastes. He likes the conservative and classical. The writers and texts he admired were well established in the canon of English literature and did not include any works written in his lifetime. He preferred literary works whose worth was generally recognized. His wife in her biography of him tells us:

> He was a great reader of the King James version of the Bible, and of the historians Carlyle and Gibbon, whose styles he greatly admired, particularly that of Gibbon whose *Decline and Fall of the Roman Empire* Shoghi Effendi was so fond of that I never remember his not having a volume of it near him in his room and usually with him when he travelled. There was a small Everyman's copy of part of it next to his bed when he died. It was his own pet bible of the English language and often he would read to me excerpts from it, interrupting himself with exclamations such as 'Oh what style; what a command of English; what rolling sentences . . .' He revelled in him and throughout Shoghi Effendi's writings the influence of his style may clearly be seen, just as the biblical English is reflected in his translations of Bahá'u'lláh's Prayers, *The Hidden Words* and Tablets.[121]

Shoghi Effendi's love for Gibbon reflects itself most clearly in the style of writing he used for his formal letters, some of which are of book length. Gibbon, whose lofty place in English letters is a given, did not appreciably influence any of Shoghi Effendi's translations. However, if one looks at Shoghi Effendi's epistolary style, shades of Gibbon are readily discernible; but discussion of this is beyond the scope of this book. It is worth mentioning, however, Shoghi Effendi's retention of eloquence, formality, beauty of expression and grandeur of tone in his translation style, features also exhibited in Gibbon's masterpiece.

The King James Bible has long been accepted as enshrining the fairest flower of English expression. Although many translations have been published since, none has been acknowledged as surpassing its brilliance, beauty and poetic expression. It is, therefore, not surprising that Shoghi Effendi should have been so enamoured of it as a model of beautiful English. Of course, he knew his life work would in large part be devoted to translating the Bahá'í writings and the King James Bible was probably his primary scriptural literary model. Although he translated the Hidden Words into Victorian English, that style itself, though not King Jamesian, was produced by writers reared on it. Certainly Victorian writers accepted the literary values of the King James translation. Such elements as beauty, elevated tone, poetic devices such as rhyme, metre, alliteration, parallelism and so on are commonly found in the corpus of Victorian greats. In other words, a translator of scripture, though in a later style of English, might well wish to retain enough biblical features to have the text recognized as scripture or to hope to evoke in the reader the appropriate responses.

Shoghi Effendi admired and read Carlyle, who, like Gibbon, is a prose writer of the highest order. Carlyle was famous as a speaker and his prose is meant to be read aloud.[122] Many of Shoghi Effendi's translations were composed out loud[123] and he knew they would be read aloud. There is a musicality in both his and Carlyle's writings. Although we do not know whether Shoghi Effendi read Carlyle out loud – and it is likely that he did – this feature of Carlyle's work must surely have appealed to him. Carlyle's facility with his medium, its attractiveness and the fact that it was used to address lofty themes and universal questions of purpose and creation no doubt increased Shoghi Effendi's interest. Carlyle's voice is loud in his work; he urges on and inspires his readers. Shoghi Effendi's voice is effaced in his works but he urges on and inspires his community. This was a primary purpose of his Guardianship and Shoghi Effendi must have taken careful notice of how Carlyle sought to achieve that end and the capacity of his words to motivate people.

As can be seen, Shoghi Effendi's tastes were conservative and he admired those works and masters whose names were firmly ensconced in the canon of English literature. He used the King James Bible as a scriptural model and the works of Gibbon and Carlyle as models of English prose. We can say that the style he uses in the Hidden Words is consonant with the general Victorian style used for translations of Middle Eastern works, similar to the general tone of language used by Nicholson, FitzGerald and others. In other words, Shoghi Effendi followed the norms of the Victorian period for artistic literature.

'With the assistance of some English friends'

There are three people known to have acted as assistants to Shoghi Effendi in his translation of the Hidden Words. These were John E. Esslemont, a Scottish physician, Ethel Rosenberg, an English painter of miniatures, and George Townshend, sometime Canon of St Patrick's Cathedral, Dublin, Archdeacon of Clonfert. All were well-educated native speakers of English from the British Isles. They assisted in different capacities, Townshend's editing work spanning all of Shoghi Effendi's translations, beginning with the Hidden Words.

Esslemont (1874–1925) was a very close friend of Shoghi Effendi and was the only one to master Persian. He had also begun to learn Arabic along with Persian when he became a Bahá'í around 1914. He was fluent in French, Spanish, German and Esperanto.[124] In 1916 he and Dr Luṭfu'lláh Ḥakím, a Persian Bahá'í physician, translated the Hidden Words into Esperanto.[125] Whether they used the English version, most likely Fareed's, or went directly from the original cannot be determined.

Esslemont assisted Shoghi Effendi with his revision of the Hidden Words in February 1925.[126] This would appear to be the revision of the 1923 translation published in 1925. Esslemont was resident in Haifa for a year beginning 21 November 1924 and by February 1925 was acting as Shoghi Effendi's English language secretary.[127] He died on 22 November 1925 from complications of tuberculosis. His literary skills are evident in his book *Bahá'u'lláh and the New Era*, a basic primer on the Bahá'í Faith since its first publication in 1923. To what degree he edited Shoghi Effendi's 1924 translation, whether he only worked on the Persian section, as he knew Persian, or edited the English of the Arabic section, cannot be determined. Apparently his was a minor role, since there is no mention of assistance on the title page of the 1925 revision.

Ethel Rosenberg (1858–1930) had 'a great knowledge of general literature. Her English was very good and her French nearly perfect'.[128] Members of the early Bahá'í community sought out her advice in matters of English 'as she herself had a very easy and pleasant style'.[129] She studied Persian but did not master it.[130] In a letter from George Townshend to Shoghi Effendi in 1926 in which he offers his assistance with matters of English style, he says 'I have been told that you invited Miss Rosenberg to Haifa to help in translating work, though (as I believe) she knows little or no Persian'.[131] Rosenberg's biographer, Robert Weinberg, however, states that she knew Persian well enough to find herself 'in the unique position of being able to translate the Master's Tablets and many of the writings as and when they became available'.[132] Weinberg says that when Rosenberg was in Haifa in 1927 'her understanding of Persian was by now very good and she and the Guardian sat together comparing Townshend's suggestions word by word with the original text'. Rosenberg, however, did not know Arabic, so it is likely her assistance here was limited to editing the English prose and not consulting the original.

We now turn to George Townshend (1876–1957) who had a scholarly and rich appreciation of English literature and an expert command of the language. He was at one time Professor of English and wrote prodigiously during his lifetime including books, pamphlets, articles and poetry. He edited all the translations of Shoghi Effendi as well as his book *God Passes By*.[133] Shoghi Effendi found in him a well-trained collaborator and man of letters.

Townshend's biographer, David Hofman, publisher, literary critic and co-religionist, says that he was 'a major literary figure, undoubtedly to take his place, one day, among those other Irishmen who form so large a company in the pantheon of English letters' and then goes on to speak of his literary achievements:

> His *oeuvre* comprises three major works, a vast number of essays, prayers, meditations, commentaries, reviews, a few poems, and his Introductions to Shoghi Effendi's *God Passes By* and edited translation of *The Dawn-Breakers: Nabíl's Narrative of the Early Days of the Bahá'í Revelation* . . . these Introductions . . . in themselves . . . would add distinction to any anthology of that most brilliant coterie, the English essayists. They are among his finest work.[134]

Hofman considers Townshend a master-essayist. Among his most distinguished essays are: 'A Kinship in Genius: The English Poet-Prophets', 'The Genius of Ireland', 'Irish Mythology', 'The Language of the Commonwealth', 'Irish Humour' and 'The Beauty of Ireland'. Of particular interest here is 'A Kinship in Genius: The English Poet-Prophets' in which the depth of his appreciation of the Romantic and nineteenth-century poets is revealed. He likens 'the romantic movement in English literature' to a 'soaring and majestic song' . . . 'The brotherhood of man, the spread of universal civilization, the happiness of nations was their joyful note, sounded by Burns and Blake in the latter half of the eighteenth century and rising to a tremendous crescendo' in 'Wordsworth, Shelley, Byron, Browning, Tennyson'.[135] It would seem fair to say that Townshend knew these poetic giants intimately and may well have tried to emulate them as literary models. This mystic poem by Townshend shows a strong sense of form and style based solidly in the nineteenth century:

> Only Beloved! With a heart on fire
> And all my longings set in one desire
> To make my soul a many-stringed lyre
> For Thy dear hand to play,

I bend beneath Thy mercy-seat and pray
That in the strength of perfect love I may
Tread with firm feet the red and mystic way
    Whereto my hopes aspire.

I have forgotten all for love of Thee
And ask no other joy from destiny
Than to be rapt within Thy unity
    And – whatso'er befall –
To hear no voice on earth but Thy sweet call,
To walk among Thy people as Thy thrall
And see Thy Beauty breathing throughout all
    Eternal ecstasy.

Lead me forth, Lord, amid the wide world's ways,
To bear to Thee my witness and to raise
The dawn song of the breaking day of days.
    Make my whole life one flame
Of sacrificial deeds that shall proclaim
The new-born glory of Thy ancient name;
And let my death lift higher yet the same
    Triumphal chant of praise![136]

The feel of this poem is nineteenth century. It reflects several of the features discussed earlier which characterize that period of literature: formality, elevation, beauty of expression, archaic words and a highly structured poetic format with its three balanced verses with eight lines each of ten syllables, except lines 4 and 8 which have six. In each verse, lines 1, 2, 3 and 8 rhyme, as do lines 4, 5, 6 and 7. We could conclude, then, that like Shoghi Effendi, Townshend had conservative tastes that leaned toward the nineteenth-century masters. Neither he nor Shoghi Effendi were in the contemporary trend of twentieth-century English letters. It would appear that Shoghi Effendi found in Townshend a literary soul-mate in taste and accomplishment.

In January 1955 Shoghi Effendi asked John Ferraby, a pilgrim to Haifa and later Hand of the Cause, to give Townshend a message. This message records Shoghi Effendi's estimation of Townshend's literary standing in the Bahá'í community:

> I want you to give a message from me to George Townshend. He must take care of himself, husband his strength, and not exhaust himself with his writing. His services are greatly valued.
> He is the best writer we have. He must be taken care of. He is the best living Bahá'í writer. It is good that in spite of his frailty he is still able to write.
> He is the pre-eminent Bahá'í writer.[137]

The high regard in which Shoghi Effendi held Townshend, who rendered his services without remuneration, is obvious. It would appear that Shoghi Effendi's deep admiration for Townshend prompted him to entrust the Hidden Words and his other translations to him for editing. We might then ask, to what degree did Townshend assist Shoghi Effendi? Is what we are reading as Shoghi Effendi's translation his own? To what extent is it Townshend's?

Townshend assisted Shoghi Effendi for a period of 18 years on almost all of his translations.[138] It should be noted that Shoghi Effendi had become an excellent writer during this time. A perusal of his later translations and other works indicate that he was a mature author.

Let us now consider whether Shoghi Effendi's translation of the Hidden Words was revised by Townshend or simply edited by him. The 1923 translation is Shoghi Effendi's original translation. In 1924 he revised it, primarily by putting capitalized words which did not refer to the Deity into lower case letters. In his 1925 revision, his emendations were considerable. This implies that his own perceptions of style and polish had been considerably refined since his earlier translation. The next revision was in 1929 and was edited by Townshend and Rosenberg. The record of Townshend's editing work on the Hidden Words is not available but Robert Weinberg notes that by the time Ethel

Rosenberg arrived in Haifa in December 1926 'a steady flow of correspondence was passing between the Guardian and George Townshend and draft translations of the *Hidden Words* were being sent backwards and forwards, surely representing the most unique and unusual collaboration in the history of any religion'.[139] It may be assumed that Shoghi Effendi again revised his 1925 edition and then submitted it to Townshend in 1926 for editing. Of course, it is possible that he simply sent him a copy of the 1925 edition but this does not seem in keeping with Shoghi Effendi's pattern of continuing to improve the Hidden Words in each subsequent revision. However, records are not available, so a comparison of changes suggested by Townshend with changes originating with Shoghi Effendi is not possible. However, comparing the 1925 edition with the one of 1929, a good portion of Shoghi Effendi's 1925 revision is retained in the later work: five out the first 19 Hidden Words (or five out of 20, including the Prologue). The number of changes are roughly the same as between the 1924 and 1925 revisions.

Shoghi Effendi always made the final decision about anything that fell under the jurisdiction of his Guardianship. This is also true of suggestions made by others regarding translation, such as the editing by Townshend of Shoghi Effendi's manuscripts. In the end, whether opinions or assistance were solicited or offered, Shoghi Effendi had the last word. Marzieh Gail, a noted Bahá'í author, states:

> Emogene Hoagg worked long hours for him typing *The Dawn-Breakers*, and sometimes she would say: 'But you can't say it that way, Shoghi Effendi!' and sometimes he would listen, and sometimes not.'[140]

David Hofman also emphasizes this point:

> . . . in relation to the work which George performed for the Guardian. No one should ever imagine for a moment that the translations into English which the Guardian made of

the sacred text were ever anything but his own. However much he turned to George for advice on syntax, 'englishing', polishing and refining of style, idiomatic usage and the like, he was the final arbiter who decided whether to adopt, reject or amend any or all of George's editorial suggestions.[141]

Finally, and most important, it is Shoghi Effendi's voice that informs his translations and his other works. Townshend's voice in his own writing is quite different. If it were otherwise, we would hear Townshend in the translations and this is not the case at all. Of course, a translator can assume the persona of the author but this is unlikely.

For these reasons the 1929 translation of the Hidden Words is considered Shoghi Effendi's work and not the work of Townshend.

5

An Introduction to the Theory of Norms

For almost as long as humans have translated, they have written commentaries about their translations and the qualities they thought a translation should evince. Until this century most such writings were found in prefaces, introductions or essays written to accompany a translation and were, therefore, written subjectively, from the standpoint of the translator's personal experiences, goals and tastes. Some of these translators, such as St Jerome and Dryden, wrote commentaries which stand out as landmarks and further sparked debate. However, Translation Studies as an objective and distinct discipline is a phenomenon of the mid-twentieth century, as it was not until 1947, when Eugene A. Nida's seminal essay on Bible translating was published, that modest Translation Studies began.

It can be said that, for various reasons, no process involving language is more complex and difficult than translation. Since translation is a manipulation of two language systems, it compounds the problems encountered in a single language. Just as no one theory has yet explained language with total success, a double phenomenon like translation is even less susceptible of complete explanation. For these and other reasons some would say that a theory of translation is impossible.

It was an assumption of pioneering theoreticians earlier in this century – who tended to be heavily schooled in linguistics and who viewed translation as primarily a linguistic transformation – that meaning in one language matched meaning in another. This was the view propounded by J. R.

Firth: the meaning of a text in a source language (SL – the original language from which the translation is being made) and the meaning in the target language (TL – the language into which the original is being rendered) is the same. In other words, the SL meaning equals the TL meaning. This view has been effectively countered by J. C. Catford:

> It is clearly necessary for translation-theory to draw upon a theory of meaning . . . In terms of the theory of meaning which we make use of here – a theory deriving largely from the views of J. R. Firth – the view that SL and TL texts 'have the same meaning' or that 'transference of meaning' occurs in translation is untenable.

> Meaning, in our view, is a property of a language. An SL text has an SL meaning, and a TL text has a TL meaning – a Russian text, for instance, has a Russian meaning (as well as Russian phonology/graphology, grammar and lexis), and an equivalent English text has an English meaning. This is necessarily the case, since, following Firth, we define *meaning* as the total network of relations entered into by any linguistic form – text, item-in-text, structure, element of structure, class, term in system – or whatever it may be.[142]

Most would agree that translation is predicated on meaning or that its most elemental aspect is meaning, that translation is involved with the transposing of meaning from one language to another.

Other elements may also be transposed, such as musicality, rhythm and rhyme, and beauty, for example. But these are auxiliary components, or, perhaps, auxiliary meanings. If primary meaning (the sense of the words) were to be removed and, for instance, rhymed and metred nonsense sounds used, the result would not be a translation. Auxiliary elements, or auxiliary meanings, are components of meaning, so to speak, or are embellishments, no matter how desirable, which spin off the essential meaning. They rest on the foundations of the primary meaning and are created by the skilful and artistic device of the literary translator by means of recreating Source Text (ST – the text in the original language from which the translation is being made) primary meaning in the Target Text (TT – the text into which the original is being rendered).

To restate, in the view of Catford we have: source language meaning as a network of relations approximating target language meaning as a network of relations. Thus a poem in the source language becomes a poem in the target language, but not exactly the same poem. Or, in cruder terms, an apple becomes an orange; both are 'fruit' but not the same. Catford's theory looks away from the assumption that a source language network of relations can become a target language network of relations in exactly the same way. The values that did become possible in the transfer from source language to target language show *equivalence*, a term indicating 'any TL form (text or portion of text) which is observed to be the equivalent of a given SL form (text or portion of text)', and *formal correspondence*, a term signifying that the 'TL category (unit, class, structure, element of structure, etc.) which can be said to occupy, as nearly as possible, the "same" place in the "economy" of the TL as the given SL category occupies in the SL', which are 'nearly always approximate'.[143] In other words, formal correspondence would be a very literal word for word and category for category transfer which would usually produce a text that is at best somewhat strange and at worst unintelligible. An equivalent text would be at the other end of the spectrum and would involve any changes necessary to plug in whatever component maintains the sense of the original. This does not, however, mean an interpretation of the original, which is a new literary work of its own simply using the original as an inspiration.

Nida, possibly the most notable figure in Translation Studies, also approaches the subject from linguistics, focusing on the field of Bible translation. However, we may assume that whatever applies to Bible translating will also apply to almost any other type of translating since, in the words of Nida, it has had

> . . . a longer tradition (it began in the third century BC), involves far more languages (1393 languages by the end of 1968), is concerned with a greater variety of cultures . . . and includes a wider range of literary types (from lyric poetry to theological discourse) than any comparable kind of translating.[144]

Nida's comments have particular relevance to the investigation of the Hidden Words since it is a scriptural text. In his book *Toward a Theory of Translating* published in 1964, Nida develops Catford's idea of equivalence, using his own terminology based on the word 'equivalence'. Nida uses the term *formal-equivalence* where Catford used *formal correspondence* and, at the other end of the spectrum, in place of Catford's *equivalence*, Nida uses *dynamic-equivalence*. Nida describes *formal-equivalence*:

> Such a formal-equivalence (or F-E) translation is basically source-oriented; that is, it is designed to reveal as much as possible of the form and content of the original message.
>
> In doing so, an F-E translation attempts to reproduce several formal elements, including: (1) grammatical units, (2) consistency in word usage, and (3) meanings in terms of the source context. The reproduction of grammatical units may consist in: (a) translating nouns by nouns, verbs by verbs, etc.; (b) keeping all phrases and sentences intact (i.e. not splitting up and readjusting the units); and (c) preserving all formal indicators, e.g. marks of punctuation, paragraph breaks, and poetic indentation.[145]

It is apparent that such an approach to source oriented translation, although surely of use in some restricted instances, would shackle and bind the translator of a literary text to such a degree that any artistic rendition would be impossible. Meaning and readability, much more artistic considerations, would be subordinated to form and structure. Although source oriented translators might argue that such an approach would most closely maintain the meaning of the text, in fact a text employing formal equivalence might retain little or no meaning. Syntax and word order might be completely disrupted in an effort to be 'faithful' to the original, resulting in the target text being undecipherable, while the literal translation of a word or collocation of words in the target text may have no sensible counterpart of itself or in context and might give an altogether different reading.

Nida defines *dynamic-equivalence* as follows:

> In contrast with formal-equivalence translations others are oriented toward dynamic equivalence. In such a translation the focus of attention is directed, not so much toward the source message, as toward the receptor response. A dynamic-equivalence (or D-E) translation may be described as one concerning which a bilingual and bicultural person can justifiably say, 'That is just the way we would say it.' It is important to realize, however, that a D-E translation is not merely another message which is more or less similar to that of the source. It is a translation, and as such must clearly reflect the meaning and intent of the source.
>
> One way of defining a D-E translation is to describe it as 'the closest natural equivalent to the source-language message' . . .
>
> . . . a D-E translation is directed primarily toward equivalence of response rather than equivalence of form . . .[146]

Nida has added a new element to Catford's definition of equivalence. His focus and attention are not just on the target text but on the response of the person perusing the target text. The response in dynamic equivalence must be natural. If a translation reads perfectly easily and does not draw attention to itself by foreign-sounding intrusions, while still maintaining fidelity to the meaning, then it manifests dynamic equivalence. Of course there are instances such as cultural allusions or physical objects not known in the target language, for example, which could not be translated without some indication that the target text might be a translation. Thus, such an idea of translation has limitations.

In his next book, *The Theory and Practice of Translation* published in 1970, Nida retained the essential definition of formal-equivalence and dynamic-equivalence but in place of the term *formal-equivalence* used *formal-correspondence*, which was Catford's original term. Nida went further than simply defining the terms and presenting how they function. He posed the primacy of dynamic-equivalence over formal-equivalence:

> Of course, persons may insist that by its very nature a dynamic equivalent translation is less 'accurate' translation, for it departs further from the forms of the original. To argue in this manner, however, is to use 'accurate' in a strictly formal sense, whereas accuracy can only be rightly determined by judging the extent to which the response of the receptor is substantially equivalent to the response of the original receptors. In other words, does the dynamic equivalent translation succeed more completely in evoking in the receptors responses which are substantially equivalent to those experienced by the original receptors? If 'accuracy' is to be judged in this light, then certainly the dynamic equivalent translation is not only more meaningful to the receptors but also more accurate. This assumes, of course, that both the formal correspondence translation and the dynamic equivalent translation do not contain any overt errors of exegesis.

In summary, then, Nida can be said to have expanded the terms formal-correspondence (previously formal-equivalence) and dynamic-equivalence by developing the concept of the importance of the receptor, or reader, of the target text and then setting out the hypothesis that a dynamically equivalent text is preferable to a formally corresponding one.

If the translator – having determined that a text in the

source system is worthy of translation, in other words, will fill a slot or need in the target literary polysystem – decides to follow the norms in the source literature appropriate to the type of work being translated, then the translation is considered, according to Gideon Toury (who follows Itamar Even-Zohar's terminology) to be an *acceptable* translation. However, if the norms of the target system are brought into play, then the translation is said to be an *adequate* translation. The poles of acceptability and adequacy are related to the concept of meaning, which is the basic configuration and keystone of any theory of translation. Thus *acceptability* equates with Catford's *formal correspondence* and Nida's *formal equivalence*. Toury's *adequacy* is synonymous with Catford's *equivalence* and Nida's *dynamic-equivalence*. It is obvious that there has been a development of the terms needed to define meaning in the source and the target systems. For the sake of clarity, let us illustrate this in Table 2:

Table 2

	Source Language	**Target Language**
Catford	formal correspondence	equivalence
Nida	formal-equivalence (now functional-equivalence)	dynamic-equivalence
Even-Zohar	acceptability	adequacy
Toury	acceptability	adequacy

I find the use of the terms *acceptability* and *adequacy* arbitrary. One can easily be substituted for the other and their meanings reversed, as they are almost synonymous. I propose, therefore, for the purposes of the discussion of norms, to use the terms that have gained currency among most theorists in the field: *formal correspondence* for the pole of the source language and *dynamic-equivalence* for the pole of the target language. Thus a translation which is source oriented is a formally corresponding translation, and one which is target oriented is a dynamically equivalent translation.

Itamar Even-Zohar is credited with creating polysystem theory as applied to literature and translation and for drawing attention to the function of norms and initiating their study. He began the discussion of polysystem theory in 1970 and has developed it since then. In an article on 'Polysystem Theory' he states:

> The idea that semiotic phenomena, i.e. sign-governed human patterns of communication (e.g. culture, language, literature, society) should be regarded as systems rather than conglomerates of disparate elements, has become one of the leading ideas of our time in most sciences of man. Thus, the positivistic collection of data, taken *bona fide* on empiricist grounds and analysed on the basis of their material substance, has been replaced by a *functional* approach based on the analysis of *relations*. Viewed as systems, it became possible to describe and explain how the various semiotic aggregates *operate*. Subsequently the way was opened to achieve what has been regarded throughout the development of modern science as the latter's supreme goal: the detection of those rules governing the diversity and complexity of phenomena rather than their registration and classification.[147]

Thus, as can be seen, Even-Zohar posits a sweeping view of literature as a dynamic of systems which operate by laws. His view of literature is neither static nor ahistorical but operational and constantly changing. He speaks of conglomerates of systems which are both synchronic and diachronic. A system is

> . . . very rarely a uni-system but is, *necessarily*, a *polysystem* – a multiple system, a system of various systems which intersect with each other and partly overlap, using concurrently different options, yet functioning as one structured whole, whose members are interdependent.[148]

Of course, the notion of literature as many systems which intersect and overlap and also move from one position in a literary system to another is a helpful point of departure for discovering how literature and translation function and for judging the Hidden Words by norms appropriate for its niche. According to Even-Zohar, literature is not a discrete, prescribed group of literary texts but many interacting groups of written material. He believes that it is misleading to consider canonized literature as the only literature worthy of discussion and critical analysis. Canonized literature comprises those works considered by the intelligentsia to have high artistic merit and to embody the cultural heritage of the community. These are the 'masterpieces'. However, we are dealing here only with literature which a religion treats as part of the English-language canon.

Non-canonized literature has different relations with the canonized literature. Further, translated literature must be considered as part of the polysystem, though it may be canonized or non-canonized. The canonized and non-canonized systems are not static but struggle with each other for position within the polysystem. The canonized literature occupies the centre of this configuration, or convergence of configurations, and the non-canonized literatures, which occupy the periphery, are in different ways governed and affected by the canonical works.

The canonized system is the innovatory component of the polysystem. If the canon of literature is not constantly developing and changing by innovation then it stagnates and petrifies and non-canonized forms will try to take its place. Thus, a stable canonized system is a changing one. The non-canonized system, in order to gain stature, adopts and emulates the standards set by the canonized system.

Let us now turn our attention to the position of translation in the literary polysystem. Translated literature can occupy a place in the canonized or non-canonized system depending on various factors. If it is canonized then it is actively part of new creative forces that determine the direction in which the literature is evolving and is part of important literary events. Ezra Pound's *Cathay Poems* is an example. However, for the most part, translations are found in the non-canonized literature.

If translated literature is non-canonized then it:

> ... constitutes a peripheral system within the polysystem, generally assuming the character of epigonic writing. In other words, in such a situation it has no influence on major processes and is modelled according to norms already conventionally established by an already dominant type. Translated literature in this case becomes a major factor of conservatism. While the contemporary original literature might go on developing new norms and models, translated literature adheres to norms which have been either recently or long before rejected by the (newly) established centre. It no longer maintains positive correlations with original writing.[149]

The Hidden Words is part of the non-canonized literature and reflects very strong elements of conservatism. Since Shoghi Effendi wished for it to be accepted in the literary polysystem, he clothed his translation in conservative language. There was no apparent attempt to create new literary forms or to break established norms. On the contrary, Shoghi Effendi deliberately chose a very conservative biblical diction in which to render the Hidden Words. In so doing, he translated the work in a way which would be expected of a translation that is non-canonized.

Norms, in sociological terms, guide behaviour that falls between 'formulated laws' and idiosyncrasies. They operate when there is more than one possible type of behaviour and are used as the criteria by which a community judges its members.

Literary norms act as constraints on a literary system, since particular norms are appropriate to certain genres of literature. Conversely, it is the breaking of norms that occur in the canonized literature that accounts for an innovatory model being introduced into the literary system. Regularities in a translation in the same type of situation indicate that norms are operative.

This is where the notion of norms impinges on the concept of the polysystem, for it is the norms that regulate, for the most part, the production of the translation. In other words, the translator will follow the commonly accepted standards of style, tone, language and form which best befit the type of translation undertaken. As to the polysystemic analysis of translated literature, it is the norms that play the most important part in the non-canonized system, where translation is usually found.

We now investigate how the Hidden Words can be said to be a paradigm case for the study of norms.

6

Norms Employed by Shoghi Effendi in the Translation of the Hidden Words

In this section we will examine the four norms Shoghi Effendi used in his translation of the Hidden Words: 1) interpretation, 2) elevation, 3) beautification and 4) euphonization. With Shoghi Effendi's translations these major norms have related subordinate norms. Further, it is important to explore the hierarchy of goals or purposes, overriding and textual, which Shoghi Effendi appears to have had, as the norms chosen from the spectrum of potential norms serve specific purposes. The functioning of the norms, whether major or subordinate, can best be understood in light of their fulfilling certain goals. The analysis of each major norm will also include a discussion of the particular goals which that norm serves.

Let us first examine some of the overriding goals or purposes of Shoghi Effendi's translation as a preliminary step to the examination of the individual norms he used.

Goals and Purposes of the Translation: Overriding and Textual

In Toury's opinion, the theoretical and descriptive aspects of Translation Studies have not been given balanced consideration, the theoretical arena receiving more research attention than the descriptive. However, every theory should be tested with actual examples. An explanation for the reticence of theoreticians to submit their theories for testing by *all* translations considered as such in the target system is that there are always exceptions. In other words, the theories proposed function on an analytical level but the actual translations, which are empirical facts, often nullify them. Obviously, source-oriented theories of translation, or *a priori* theories of translation, or non-translation, as may be the case, are much easier to handle. This is not surprising if we accept the assertion that translation is the most challenging of intellectual pursuits. Most theories of translation cluster about the source pole and whatever does not fit its notion of what translation should be is termed a 'non-translation'. This may be a solution of convenience for an intellectual dilemma but it is no real solution. It simply delays the development of viable translation theories, if in fact such an accomplishment is possible. However, we cannot deny the very real existence of translations that are accepted as such in the target pole and serve a particular intended function. A translation is a translation, whether so called or not. Thus it can be seen why, among other reasons, a source pole theoretic framework has been most popular. Nevertheless, Toury and others postulate the need for a target pole theoretical system to explain translation as a phenomenon of relationships accepted as such in the target system. In addition, a descriptive branch of Translation Studies needs to be established for appraising such theories.[150] It is from this perspective that the following discussion is offered. It presents some new concepts in the understanding and description of the goals and purposes of the translator and considers how these are reflected in the norms utilized to render a work. These ideas were developed from analyses of Shoghi Effendi's translation of the Hidden Words.

That translation is a teleological process has been long acknowledged but generally so only in passing, as the point is so obvious that any in-depth attempt at describing it would have no merit. However, in the words of Toury:

. . . the exertion of any single act of translating is to a large extent conditioned by the goal it serves. Thus, in order to be able to understand the process of translation and its products, one should first determine the purposes which they are meant to serve, and these purposes are set mainly by the target, receptor pole which, in processes of this type, serves as the 'initiator' of the inter-textual, inter-cultural and interlingual transfer . . .[151]

We shall describe the hierarchy of goals and then illustrate their application with the Hidden Words. Let us begin with an elucidation of two terms I have developed, the concepts of overriding and textual goals and purposes. The term *overriding goals* or *purposes* specifies those aspirations that impel one's overall actions, those motivations that are personal or direct a part of, or the totality of, one's life or work. In other words, the overriding goal is not textual; it directs the translator's actions and impels him in a particular direction. Using Shoghi Effendi as an example, overriding goals are those larger issues to which the translation of the Hidden Words is subordinate. To put it another way, the overriding goals are the reasons the Hidden Words was translated and why it was translated in the way it was. If postulated as a hierarchy of goals and purposes, these would be uppermost.

Let us now illustrate the overriding purposes which appear to have guided Shoghi Effendi's life and work. It should be remembered that Shoghi Effendi was not an ordinary translator; he was the head of the Bahá'í Faith and its authorized Expounder. Thus his exposition of the meaning of any of the Bahá'í writings (and translation as exposition) stands as equally binding on Bahá'ís as the original texts themselves. This most important function was a primary responsibility of many responsibilities, far too many to cite; therefore, only the most obvious functions are described, along with those whose impact in moulding the particular textual goals are easily seen.

In addition to being Expounder of these texts, Shoghi

Effendi was the head of a religion with world-embracing aspirations and which had at his death in 1957 literally circled the globe with adherents in many countries. He provided devotional texts for the believers and inspired Bahá'ís around the world to spread the teachings of Bahá'u-'lláh and to establish Bahá'í communities. He also urged them to embody the virtues set down in the Bahá'í scriptures. Since a great deal of personal hardship and sacrifice was being asked of Bahá'ís in these efforts, they needed scripture that would inspire, solace and sustain them. In addition, it seems Shoghi Effendi believed that it was in the best interests of the Bahá'í community for its sacred texts to be couched in language that would last for as long a period of time as possible.

Subservient to these overriding goals are what may be termed *textual goals* or *purposes*. These textual goals serve the overriding purposes but rather than being general in nature and directing the course of one's life, they are particular to the text and serve specific functions in creating a certain kind of text that will fit into and be in harmony with the overall schemata of goals and purposes of which they form a part.

The textual goals and purposes of the Hidden Words that may be discerned are:

1. TO INSPIRE (TO ACTION)

Scripture has always inspired people and this is one of the expectations a scriptural text needs to fulfil in order to be accepted as such. Therefore it is not surprising to find this as a textual goal of the Hidden Words.

2. TO IMBUE WITH SPIRITUAL FEELING (PATHOS)

This textual goal deals with an intangible emotion, which can only be explained subjectively. However, it can be argued that such pathos stems from the particular nature of scripture, a result of which devotees of other scriptures would, most probably, be aware. However, many would argue that this is not attainable from the nature of the translation but is inherent in the text itself. In other words, the pathos is, by definition, part of the source text and needs to be retained in the translation.

3. To make enduring

This textual goal is logical in that the limited resources of the Bahá'í Faith make retranslation of the Hidden Words within a fairly short span of years problematic. Further, some time would necessarily elapse before the translations of Shoghi Effendi, which are also considered interpretation, would be sufficiently assimilated and understood by Bahá'í scholars and translators to enable them successfully to translate other original Bahá'í texts. Shoghi Effendi's translations were meant to be a model for other translations and to stand for some time.

4. To make grand (grandeur)

The sense of grandeur implied here is being high in rank, magnificent, splendid, impressive and stately; there is no pretention intended. Since scripture is considered as coming from on high, it is understandable that a scriptural text should reflect the highest rank of written expression possible.

5. To make elegant (or to ornament)

This goal implies the highest meaning of elegance and ornamentation. The text is considered to be of the utmost importance and therefore should be rendered beautifully, ornamentation being one standard of beauty. However, this is not intended in the sense of over-ornamentation for its own sake, overwhelming the text with tasteless and excessive decoration.

6. TO MAKE ELOQUENT

This textual goal seeks to set the text at a lofty level of speech, distinguished from the unlovely or ordinary prose of most written material.

If we subserve these goals to the overriding principles, we might say that the textual purposes of 'to inspire' and 'to imbue with spiritual feeling' would fall primarily under the overriding goals of sustaining the flock and exhorting them to a rectitude of conduct. To provide texts that do not soon need retranslating, the textual goal of 'to make enduring' needs to be met. In other words, a conservative, or even somewhat archaic, style of English would be appropriate for a scriptural text intended to last for a considerable period of time, whereas similar work in the vernacular would need to be revised frequently to keep up with changes in the spoken language. The textual purposes of 'to make grand', 'to make elegant' and 'to make eloquent' dignify the text and lend it credibility, thus rendering it more readily acceptable to new English-speaking Bahá'ís and facilitating the spread of the religion, an overriding goal of Shoghi Effendi.

A feature of these textual goals is that they are quite general. It is the norms which distil the generality of these concepts in specificity.

Table 3

Hierarchy of Goals and Purposes of Shoghi Effendi

Overriding Goals	Textual Goals
To interpret the Bahá'í writings	To inspire To imbue with spiritual feeling To make enduring
To sustain believers	To inspire To imbue with spiritual feeling

126

Table 3 (continued...)

Hierarchy of Goals and Purposes of Shoghi Effendi

Overriding Goals	*Textual Goals*
To provide text for devotional purposes	To inspire To imbue with spiritual feeling To make grand To make elegant To make eloquent
To spread the religion	To make grand To make elegant To make eloquent
To provide lasting translations	To make enduring
To provide translations stylistically acceptable as scripture	To make grand To make elegant To make eloquent

As indicated in Table 3, there is much overlapping of textual goals in that they serve more than one objective, indeed several. A complex picture emerges of the interrelationships of the elements, which intensifies when norms are introduced. It is to them we now turn our attention.

Hierarchy of Literary Norms and Related Concepts

Toury states that translation is a complex interchange between two languages and two literary traditions, each with its system of norms. He posits a 'value' underlying translation, composed of two components: 1) being a worthwhile text to fill an appropriate 'slot' in the target literary polysystem', and 2) being a translation of a particular source text in the source polysystem which fills a certain position within that polysystem. Of this situation, Toury comments:

Thus, this 'value' contains requirements deriving from two essentially different sources, often incompatible, if not diametrically opposed to one another . . . This is the main reason for the high complexity of the picture revealed when one approaches the field of translational norms, in theory as well as in actual research.[152]

Thus, in the first instance, the text must fill a need in the target system. We might conclude from this that an arbitrary translation which fills no need in the target system would create a scenario of confusion in that there would be no clear-cut direction to follow in choosing the norms appropriate to it. Secondly, it must be a translation representing one literary text in another literary system. Pseudo-translations – original literary works written in the target language which pretend to be translations so as to be acceptable – do not meet the second criterion. These are usually innovative and break the norms expected for their particular type of text. However, as something exotic, imported from another language and culture, they may find acceptance as alleged translations.

Let us now examine the Hidden Words in light of these two criteria. For Bahá'ís, the Hidden Words is among the most important texts written in Arabic. In Arabic Bahá'í literature it is, after the Kitáb-i-Aqdas (Most Holy Book) and the Kitáb-i-Íqán (Book of Certitude) the most important book in the Bahá'í corpus of literature. Its value being very high, it is quite understandable that Shoghi Effendi chose to translate it.

The second criterion, however, poses some problems. The corpus of Arabic literature is largely 'Islamic' literature or, at least, literature not incongruent with Islamic society. Bahá'u'lláh's works – except for a very few examples, such as some poetry – are not considered to be literature; rather, they are considered heretical works which, had the religious and the governmental authorities been able to carry out their designs of almost a century and a half, would be completely obliterated and destroyed. Thus the Bahá'í writings, of which the Hidden Words is a part, have a negative value in Muslim societies, although to the Bahá'ís living in those countries their value is beyond estimation. Further, those works that have been translated into English (and thence into hundreds of other languages) are also of the highest value to Bahá'ís around the world, including those who can read the original texts. The phenomenon of a conflicting value assigned to a literary work I call a *relative value*. In other words, if we view literature in the usual dichotomy of canonized versus non-canonized, or primary versus secondary systems, we will usually be easily able to define a work's value in that system. This is because the society as a whole, for the most part, follows the predilections of its critics and belletrists as to what is 'high' literature and what is not. There is usually no public outcry accompanied by fanatic sentiments which seeks to obliterate a segment of that literary system, except perhaps pornography and underground political resistance literature, which the state often wishes to eradicate but which finds enough popular support to exist nonetheless. However, Bahá'í literature does face this response in some Muslim lands. Bahá'í communities in Islamic countries are small, where they exist at all, and cannot at this time countermand the censure of such works as the Hidden Words. Thus the term *relative value* is added to Toury's *value* to clarify further the processes moulding the basic concept of what comprises a translation.

As for the actual process of translation, norms function at every level. Toury begins with the concept of *preliminary norms*, which has two sub-sections:

> *Preliminary norms* have to do with two main sets of consider-ations: those regarding the very existence of a definite translation 'policy' along with its actual nature, and those questions related to the 'directness' of translation.
>
> As 'considerations regarding translation policy' I have in mind the factors affecting or determining the choice

of works (or at least of authors, genres, schools, source literatures [sic], and the like to be translated . . .

Considerations concerning directness of translation involve the threshold of tolerance for translating from languages other than SL: is an intermediate (second-hand) translation permitted at all? In translating from what (primary) source literatures/literary systems/periods and the like is it permitted/prohibited/tolerated/preferred? . . .

It is reasonable to assume that certain relationships hold between these two sets of norms. But they are by no means fixed and given.[153]

The first consideration regards the policy determining the choice of works, authors, literatures and so on. Shoghi Effendi's obligations as Guardian of the Bahá'í Faith left no room for translating texts other than the Bahá'í writings, except for the history of the Bábís, *The Dawn-Breakers*. He chose the most important works to translate at the time and also included those excerpts from the Arabic and Persian which would best illustrate points in his own correspondence and in his only book, *God Passes By*. All these are replete with translations ranging from a phrase to several pages.

As for the second consideration regarding directness of translation, Shoghi Effendi translated only from the original Arabic and Persian writings of the Báb, Bahá'u'lláh and 'Abdu'l-Bahá. He confined himself to this corpus, except for the above-mentioned *Dawn-Breakers*. It is interesting here to note that Shoghi Effendi chose English as the medium for his translations from this body of work, possibly presaging the continued growth of English as a world language and its predominance among the second languages learned in many countries.

Toury's next category is *operational norms*, which affect the process of the manipulation of larger segments of the text and also the linguistic material in the translation. Thus this category is divided into two sections: *matricial norms* and *textual norms*.

Matricial norms determine (or at least highly affect) the very *existence* of TL material . . . its *location* in the text (or the form of actual distribution) and the *textual segmentation* . . . They also determine the extent to which such omissions, additions, changes in location, and manipulation of segmentation are openly referred to in the translated works themselves (by means of statements such as abridged, adapted, and the like). Obviously, the borderlines between these matricial phenomena are not clear-cut. For instance, omission on a large scale often produces changes in segmentation as well; a change in location may also be described as an omission (in one place) plus an addition (somewhere else,) [sic] and so on.

Textual (proper) norms affect or determine the actual selection of TL material (units and patterns) to replace the original textual and linguistic material, or (as we assume that the very concept of translation in its modern sense implies some equivalence postulate) to serve as translational equivalents to it. Textual norms may be either purely linguistic (including general stylistic norms) or literary (determining, for instance, what is appropriate for literature in general, for a translated literary work, for a certain genre/literary source/period, for a certain literary technique, and so forth).[154]

The matricial norms affect the arrangement of the text and also cover 'omissions, additions, changes in location, and manipulation of segmentation'. Applying this to the Hidden Words, Shoghi Effendi could have abridged or condensed it had he chosen, or arranged it differently on the page. However, he chose to keep the general textual segmentation which had been inaugurated by the previous translators, perhaps because people had become accustomed to it or it could not be improved upon.

A word is in order here regarding the arrangement of the original text, which is kept at the International Bahá'í Archives in Haifa, Israel. Following Middle Eastern custom, the different segments are written in various directions on the page. There is no punctuation, as this was not a convention in Arabic literature at the time; even today Arabic punctuation follows few codified rules and is often haphazard at best. Thus it seems that the first known translator into English of a major portion of the Hidden Words, Kheiralla, arranged them in an order typical of the English literary system and added suitable punctuation. Numbering was added by Amin Fareed. Stannard altered Fareed's numbering slightly by omitting numbers for the Prologue and Epilogue. Shoghi Effendi kept this innovation. In other words, we might say that Shoghi Effendi generally kept the matricial norms as established and developed by the earlier translators, although he put the Prologue and Epilogue into italics.

Now let us examine the textual or proper norms. These determine the actual material on the page and also can be said to provide an equivalence postulate. Thus sentences, paragraphs and so on in the target text are said to replace or have some, if not all, relations to the same, or some of the same, elements in the source text. (This area of norms will be dealt with at length in the section on the specific norms found in the Hidden Words.) This category may be further subdivided into *major* and *subordinate norms*. The reason for this is that the category of textual norms is not specific enough to account for various translation phenomena observed in the course of my research on the Hidden Words. Only a further distillation of hierarchies of norms explains why certain norms overlap or can only be expressed in general terms. For example, the four textual or proper norms initially found in this investigation were interpretation, elevation, beautification and euphonization. Other norms struggled for independent identification but were dismissed. However, this arrangement was not intellectually satisfactory and was, indeed, at times puzzling. Therefore, the four textual norms first isolated are called *major norms* while those which fall under them are termed *subordinate norms*. Placing these subordinate norms under the major ones explains their functions more clearly. This paradigm is far more satisfying than the previous briefer construct.

There is one more concept of Toury's which should be explored: the *initial norm*. Toury defines this as follows:

This most important notion is a useful means to denote the translator's basic choice between two polar alternatives deriving from the two major constituents of the 'value' in literary translation mentioned earlier: he subjects himself either to the original text, with its textual relations and the norms expressed by it and contained in it, or to the linguistic and literary norms active in TL and in the target literary polysystem, or a certain section of it . . .

If the first position is adopted, as an overall strategy, or concerning certain parts or even only details, the translation tends to adhere to the norms of the original work, and through them – as well – to the norms of SL and/or the source literary polysystem as a whole. This tendency, which we shall call . . . the pursuit of an *adequate translation* may mean – or cause – incompatibility of the translated text with the target linguistic and/or literary norms . . .

If, on the other hand, the second position is adopted, the operational linguistic and literary norms of the target system are triggered and set into full operation. Whereas adherence to the norms of the original determines its *acceptability* in the target linguistic and/or literary polysystems as well as its exact position within them.

It is only reasonable to assume, of course, that in practice the decision made will generally be some combination of (or compromise between) these two extremes . . . In my opinion, this is one of the best interpretations of the common argument that translation, especially literary translation, always involves an encounter, if not a confrontation, between two sets of norms . . .[155]

The concept of 'initial norm', which Toury has named as such for lack of a better term, brings us squarely back to the notion of equivalence, not in binary terms but as the polar alternatives of source and target poles and all intersections intervening in between. The initial norm might have just as well been termed the *equivalence postulate norm* or the *pole norm* (meaning oriented towards the source or target pole). However, even though 'initial norm' is very much like 'primary norm', we shall retain Toury's designation.

Basically, it is here that the translator must choose at what point in the continuum between source and target poles he wishes to place the translation. Such a consideration is coloured by the type of translation, the place it will fill in the target system, and other considerations. As described above, this does not produce a translation which is uniformly reflective of one point along the source–target continuum but may be a very complex intermingling of elements, some oriented more to the target pole and some oriented more to the source pole. However, usually a translation can be placed generally somewhere in one camp or the other. The confrontation from such an encounter is most aptly put above as engaging the differing sets of norms.

Let us now turn to Shoghi Effendi and how he seems to have resolved this situation. Since the Hidden Words is for Bahá'ís a scriptural text, Shoghi Effendi had certain limitations. First of all, meaning was paramount; any translation of sacred text must, above all, retain the meaning insofar as possible. After this overriding obligation, stylistic preferences may be pursued. A literal rendition would be source-oriented and most probably clumsy. However, in light of Shoghi Effendi's overriding goal 'to provide a translation stylistically acceptable as scripture' he would have to produce a target-oriented translation. Shoghi Effendi had a strong sense of English style and of the norms appropriate to English literary forms. He appears to have striven to produce the most stylistically acceptable translation possible while still maintaining fidelity to the content of the original. We might say, then, that Shoghi Effendi leaned heavily towards what would be a target-oriented translation. That is, his initial norm would direct him to rend the Hidden Words in English in such as way as to make it most readily accepted as a scriptural work. In line with his own literary predilections, Shoghi Effendi strove to make his translation as dignified and stately as possible. By examining the norms he employed, we shall see how he put this initial norm into practice.

The hierarchy of norms as discussed above is depicted in Table 4.

Table 4

Hierarchy of Norms

Value

Relative Value

Preliminary Norms

Operational Norm

Matricial

Initial

Major

Subordinate

Procedures for Investigation

If the constraints which impinge on the production of a translation of a literary text are constructed as a hierarchy, we would find four levels, as follows in Table 5:

Table 5

Hierarchy of Constraints

1 Formal Constraints
   (e.g. sound patterns, grammatical rules)

2 Intersubjective Constraints
   (models, norms)

3 Subjective Constraints
   (personal taste, idiosyncracies)

4 Ideological Constraints

In trying to identify the norms, the researcher must distinguish between data from these four levels. The first level of formal constraints is easily dismissed, since there is no allowable deviation by the language system for the translator to manipulate – with the exception of poetic licence – the creation of new words or alteration of spelling for metrical reasons, for example. Except in unusual instances, there is little room for this in translation and we will not be concerned with this first category, as data belonging to it can be readily identified and is of no consequence. The first level, then, is considered to be a 'low level' of constraint, as there is little activity which is not predetermined. In other words, there are few choices.

As for the second category, intersubjective constraints, it is here the norms are placed, and this is the sphere of our investigative activity. It is the 'high level' of constraint as there are many alternatives from which to choose. However, it can be a challenge to ferret out norms as opposed to personal taste or idiosyncracies, which are intersubjective constraints on the text. The distinguishing factor of a norm is its repetition in the text, and in order for it to be designated as such, it must be repeatedly utilized by the translator. If a translation device does not recur, then it may well be an indication of the subjective taste of the translator being acted upon in that instance or simply an idiosyncracy for which no rationale can be given. Idiosyncratic behaviour can be attributed to such human factors as fatigue or misreading the source text. Thus in determining and isolating the norms which fall in the middle ground as intersubjective constraints, repetition is the watchword. If there is no recurring pattern, the phenomenon observed may be indicative of subjective constraints and, therefore, not identifiable as a norm.

The fourth category, ideological constraints, indicates the influence that a certain set of beliefs, or ideology, has on the production of the translation which might impel the translator to rewrite the target text to some degree. This particular constraint is only operative in certain types of translation, such as of political or religious texts. It is possible such manoeuvres would be utilized by a translator of religious texts who is taking a particular theological position and in which corruption of the original content would lead to some gain. Since the Hidden Words is a mystical work, it is not the type of work likely to be tampered with by a translator, much less by Shoghi Effendi, of whom such behaviour would be out of character.

It might well be asked, however, whether Shoghi Effendi was influenced by certain beliefs when he translated the Hidden Words. There is no doubt that his profound understanding of the Bahá'í writings, instilled in him from childhood, helped clarify his understanding of the source text. He, therefore, was in an ideal position to perceive the meaning of the original, which is not by any means a simple text to comprehend. My examination of the Hidden Words has revealed no bending of the essential meaning.

However, the reverse question might be more relevant: how did Shoghi Effendi's interpretation and, hence, translation of the Hidden Words affect the belief system of his religion? Since he was, as Guardian, the only one in the Bahá'í Faith after 'Abdu'l-Bahá authorized to interpret the Bahá'í corpus, his interpretations stand for Bahá'ís as clarification and elucidation of the various texts he either translated or discussed, including the Hidden Words. In this way he has helped to shape the understanding and comprehension of the teachings of the Bahá'í Faith.

Norms are also called 'policies', the word 'policy' implying guidance on a course of action in a particular situation; norms or policies are most easily identified when they are put in the form of a command. Thus if repeated behaviour can be rephrased in terms of an instruction, admonition or command, it is a policy or norm. In the subsequent discussion of the major and subordinate norms, the norms will be identified in their command form, such as 'beautify the text', as well as in the simpler description 'beautification'.

The translator is not always conscious of a norm but if there is a high frequency of repetition, there probably is awareness on the part of the translator. Since Shoghi Effendi was greatly enamoured of the English language and had studied it for most of his life, and in light of the overriding goals discussed earlier, it is hard to imagine that he was not aware of the norms he employed. The major norms of interpretation, elevation, beautification and euphonization are also found in his other translations of the Bahá'í corpus, and so it is safe to assume that there was a very conscious and deliberate infusion of these norms into the Hidden Words. Also, because he had a highly analytical mind, it is hard to imagine that Shoghi Effendi made his translation with any-thing but intent introspection and meticulous attention.

There may be contradictory norms, which are more likely to arise in an unstable period in the literary polysystem when the norms are changing and in a state of flux. Since Shoghi Effendi chose to render the Hidden Words in a conservative style of English, there was no such unstable situation and his rendition does not display any such observable contradic-tions.

It is not necessary to peruse every page of a text to dis-cover the norms employed by the translator. For the experi-enced researcher, three to five pages may be sufficient; ten pages should be ample for a novel. There are 71 Hidden Words in Arabic plus the Prologue. I have examined 18 of these (numbers 1, 2, 3, 4, 5, 7, 8, 10, 12, 13, 14, 21, 22, 23, 24, 48, 49 and 50) and the Prologue – that is, over a quarter of the text – and have illustrated these in chart form (see chapter 7). From this analysis we can determine the norms used in Shoghi Effendi's translation of the Hidden Words.

The Major Norm of Interpretation

The major norm of interpretation can also be stated as 'to interpret the text'. The interpretation of the Bahá'í texts, here the Hidden Words, was a primary duty of Shoghi

Effendi. This particular norm is the only major norm that overlaps any of the overriding goals, discussed earlier. In Table 3, above, the first overriding goal is 'to interpret the Bahá'í writings', which coincides with the major norm of interpretation. By 'interpretation' is not meant the usual type of interpretation of a text that any translator necessarily must undertake and, indeed, is part and parcel of the very act of translation. Rather, it means that Shoghi Effendi's translations are infused with authority in the eyes of the Bahá'ís. If we consider the first translators of the Hidden Words, their translations were, presumably, the best they could produce, or at the very least, they made a sincere effort within the parameters of their capacity; but there was no stamp of authority upon them. Even though 'Abdu'l-Bahá was living when the translations of Kheiralla, Fareed and Stannard were rendered, there was never any indication that these translations were authoritative. No particular translation was cited as being primary or superior. They were always appreciated but none had official sanction. On the contrary, 'Abdu'l-Bahá, speaking about translations of Bahá'í writings in the future, said, 'At that time Tablets will be translated correctly and published. What ye have in your hands and what is already printed will impart a certain degree of information.'[156] Although this is an excerpt from a Tablet written in 1906, 'Abdu'l-Bahá never contradicted it. Kheiralla and Fareed's translations were completed by this time, Fareed's being the one in common use by Bahá'ís. Stannard showed 'Abdu'l-Bahá the proofs of her translation and she asked for interpretation of some abstruse points. These few comments, as answers to questions, are contained in the Appendix of her translation and comprise three and a quarter pages. However, they do not address translation problems but are rather theological elucidations. Therefore, even though Stannard was in contact with 'Abdu'l-Bahá, who also penned a line of appreciation for her service, she had no particular authorization for her translation.

It was to Shoghi Effendi that 'Abdu'l-Bahá gave the authority to interpret the texts of the Bahá'í writings in his capacity as Expounder and Guardian, in preparation for which 'Abdu'l-Bahá had groomed Shoghi Effendi from early childhood. It is for this reason that Bahá'ís view his translations differently from the translations done by others. Thus the normal function of interpretation, which defines part of the process of translation, overlaps in Shoghi Effendi's particular case with his designation as official, authorized interpreter. In line with the importance of this facet of his work, interpretation as a major norm is presented first.

The primary policy of Shoghi Effendi as Expounder, then, is to clarify and interpret the work so that there is no mistaking the meaning, so elemental to a scriptural text. Maintaining the meaning free from corruption is paramount. The Hidden Words, however, presents some challenges in comprehension because it is a mystical work and by nature has many levels of meaning. It is not an easy text to understand, much less to translate accurately. It should be noted that the use of the word 'accurate' in this analysis is used in Nida's sense:

> Since words cover areas of meaning and are not mere points of meaning, and since in different languages the semantic areas of corresponding words are not identical, it is inevitable that the choice of the right word in the receptor language to translate a word in the source-language text depends more on the context than upon a fixed system of verbal consistency, i.e. always translating one word in the source language by a corresponding word in the receptor language.[157]

Shoghi Effendi does not use only one word or phrase to translate an item unless it refers to a specific concept or thing in the Bahá'í framework that would justify it, as in the Prologue (line 6) where 'Covenant of God' is capitalized and refers to a particular idea and not to anything else. Shoghi Effendi does not slavishly translate one element from the source language into the exact corresponding element in the target language. Thus a verb need not be translated by a verb, nor a clumsy-sounding but closely equivalent word in meaning replace the same word in the source text. There is a flexibility in Shoghi Effendi's translation which creates a work that maintains all the elements of the original such as content, beauty and music. His translation is a composite: content is the primary consideration but no other aspect is sacrificed on the altar of literalness. Since Shoghi Effendi was not only the translator of the Hidden Words but its authorized interpreter, perhaps he felt it especially necessary to retain in his rendition the totality of the original insofar as it was possible.

Let us now examine a clear instance of the norm of interpretation found in Hidden Word Arabic 1.

١   ۞(يَا ابْنَ الرُّوحِ)۞

فِى أَوَّلِ الْقَوْلِ أَمْلِكْ قَلْباً جَيِّداً حَسَناً

مُنِيرِ الِتَمْلِكَ مُلْكاً دَائِماً بَاقِياً أَزَلاً قَدِيماً

O SON OF SPIRIT!

1   My first counsel is this: Possess a pure, kindly and
2   radiant heart, that thine may be a sovereignty ancient,
3   imperishable and everlasting.

The phrase فى اول القول which opens this Hidden Word reads in the Arabic as a statement, loosely: 'in the first saying' or 'the first statement (is)'. Shoghi Effendi interpreted this phrase by changing it to the command mode: 'My first counsel is this.' In other words, it is not simply a statement that opens the Hidden Words but a condition for proceeding on a spiritual odyssey, the Hidden Words purporting to be a guidebook, so to speak, for such a journey. It commands one first to have a 'pure, kindly and radiant heart' before going forward.

Let us now look at some other examples of interpretation from Hidden Word Arabic 2:

141

٢ *(يَا ابْنَ الرُّوحِ)*

أَحَبُّ الأَشْيَاءِ عِنْدِي الأَنْصَافُ
لا تَرْغَبْ عَنْهُ إِنْ تَكُنْ إِلَيَّ رَاغِبًا وَلا
تَغْفُلْ مِنْهُ لِتَكُونَ لِي أَمِينًا وَأَنْتَ تُوَفَّقُ بِذٰلِكَ
أَنْ تُشَاهِدَ الأَشْيَاءَ بِعَيْنِكَ لا بِعَيْنِ الْعِبَادِ
وَتَعْرِفَهَا بِمَعْرِفَتِكَ لا بِمَعْرِفَةِ أَحَدٍ فِي الْبِلَادِ
فَكِّرْ فِي ذٰلِكَ كَيْفَ يَنْبَغِي أَنْ يَكُونَ
ذٰلِكَ مِنْ عَطِيَّتِي عَلَيْكَ وَعِنَايَتِي لَكَ
فَاجْعَلْهُ أَمَامَ عَيْنَيْكَ

O SON OF SPIRIT!

1   The best beloved of all things in My sight is Justice;
2   turn not away therefrom if thou desirest Me
3   and neglect it not that I may confide in thee.
4   By its aid thou shalt see with thine own eyes and
5   not through the eyes of others, and shalt know of
6   thine own knowledge and not through the knowledge
7   of thy neighbour. Ponder this in thy heart;
8   how it behoveth thee to be. Verily justice is My
9   gift to thee and the sign of My loving-kindness. Set
10   it then before thine eyes.

In line 3 is found the following: 'and neglect it not that I may confide in thee'. The phrase 'that I may confide in thee' clarifies the Arabic لتكون لى امينًا (lit. 'that you may be trustworthy with me'). Only one who is trustworthy can be confided in (and, of course, can do other things too). So here Shoghi Effendi takes the prerogative to indicate just what is meant by this.

In line 9 the word عناية, which has the first dictionary meaning in the Arabic of 'concern; interest' and, particularly, 'divine solicitude', is translated as 'loving-kindness'. This word choice clarifies the intention of the original by making it more specific and descriptive than the broader terms

142

'concern' or 'interest' and more readable than 'divine solicitude'; it is a concern that embraces love and kindness.

In the first line the Arabic word عندي, which means 'I have' or 'with me', is rendered as 'in My sight' by Shoghi Effendi. This word is actually a particle in Arabic grammar with a suffixed personal pronoun. Such a combination with the exact implications is not found in English. So it has apparently been interpreted as 'in My sight', which implies a point of view on the part of the Divinity.

Let us now investigate the hierarchy of major and subordinate norms as they pertain to the major norm of interpretation. The major norms may be carried out or implemented by using certain policies. I have called these policies *subordinate norms*. The subordinate norms observed are noted in the Norm Chart in chapter 7. However, it has not been possible to isolate subordinate norms for every major norm. Nor, indeed, are all norms apparent. Sometimes there are simply unanswered questions.

Under the major norm of interpretation is the subordinate norm of addition, which can also be stated as 'add to the text elements necessary for equivalence', as seen in Hidden Word Arabic 3 (line 1):

$$ ٣ \quad *(يَا ابْنَ الْإِنْسَانِ)* $$

$$ كُنْتُ فِى قِدَمِ ذَاتِى وَ أَزَلِيَّةِ كَيْنُونَتِى $$

$$ عَرَفْتُ حُبِّى فِيْكَ خَلَقْتُكَ وَ أَلْقَيْتُ عَلَيْكَ $$

$$ مِثَالِى وَ أَظْهَرْتُ لَكَ جَمَالِى $$

O SON OF MAN!
1 Veiled in My immemorial being and in the ancient
2 eternity of My essence, I knew My love for thee;
3 therefore I created thee, have engraved on thee
4 Mine image and revealed to thee My beauty.

Two words have been added by Shoghi Effendi in his interpretation of this Hidden Word: neither 'veiled' nor 'ancient' are found in the Arabic. However, although these particular words are not in the original, they fill out the meaning and make the passage more comprehensible even though the phrase is obscure in both languages. The Arabic phrase فى قدم ذاتى might be taken literally to mean 'in the infinite pre-existence of my self'. Shoghi Effendi translated this as 'in My immemorial being' which maintains the sense of eternal time and pre-existence without sounding heavy-handed. This rendition is also more clear, as 'infinite pre-existence or timelessness of God' is not readily comprehended. To this phrase Shoghi Effendi adds the word 'veiled', which presents another dimension to the understanding of 'My immemorial being'. Through the use of the word 'veiled' Shoghi Effendi modifies the phrase by adding to it the concept of God being veiled from the comprehension of men. He has been veiled from us in His immemorial being. That is, His immemorial being is a place to which no man has access; it is unknowable but has always existed. By the use of the subordinate norm of addition, Shoghi Effendi, as observed in this example, has utilized addition of a linguistic element not found in the original to interpret this phrase.

The phrase following this in the Arabic is ازلية كينونتى, which can be translated as 'the eternity of My essence (or being)'. Shoghi Effendi has used the subordinate norm of addition to add the word 'ancient' as a modification of 'eternity', thus: 'ancient eternity of My essence'. The word 'eternity' has implications of future as well as past time. Here the emphasis is on the past, the 'ancient eternity' of time in which God created man, since man is a fact of being in the present and not something anticipated in the future.

These are two instances where the major norm of interpretation is further served by the use of the subordinate norm of addition as a tool to chisel out the meaning and clarify the respective passages.

Interpretation is also found side by side with the other major norms, and as this discussion continues, further interrelationships with major and subordinate norms will be presented. For now, however, we initiate the investigation of the major norm of elevation.

The Major Norm of Elevation

The major norm of elevation can also be stated as a policy: 'elevate the tone of the language to befit Holy Writ'. This norm is in congruence with the overriding goals noted above. In English-speaking societies there have traditionally been certain expectations of a text which purports to be scripture. For several centuries and into the present one an archaic English style of writing, reserved particularly for the Bible, has been considered the only suitable vehicle to carry writing of sacred origin. However, the tendency now is for new translations of the Bible to be couched in the vernacular or varying degrees of it. Nonetheless, the King James Version, which uses the most archaic language, also remains standard, and, in fact, many people prefer it because they consider it the most beautiful rendition although they might not fully understand its language.

It is not surprising that Shoghi Effendi chose an antiquated style of language for his translation of the Hidden Words. Such a version would fulfil some of the objectives towards which he was working. A text rendered in such language would evoke in its readers feelings of reverence reserved for sacred texts. Thus the translation might then sustain the believers and inspire them because it would be imbued with spiritual feeling. Of course, we can, admittedly, argue that such a posture on the part of the reader emanates primarily from the content of the text, but that effect could be substantially diminished if the tenor and style employed are mundane rather than reverent. Thus the goal of providing a stylistically acceptable scripture is served. A scriptural work that utilizes a biblical style would probably be more readily accepted by new Western converts, as such a rendition would be considered more credible and prestigious.

As was mentioned previously, in a literary system with a long literary tradition, a translation, as part of the target non-canonized system, will usually employ norms already established by the canonized system, since it seeks to be

accepted by the target readers. Thus in an attempt to legiti-
mize itself, translation in such a system is conservative.
Shoghi Effendi, in keeping with this characteristic, clothed
the Hidden Words and his other translations in a conservative, biblical style, though not one imitative of the King
James Bible. As discussed previously, Shoghi Effendi used
a Victorian English style or, at least, language with Victorian
overtones such as would be found in nineteenth-century
translations of the Qur'án, Middle Eastern poetry and wisdom literature and original English poetry with Eastern
motifs. Shoghi Effendi translated the Hidden Words in the
third decade of the twentieth century, and that style of
English was still employed by translators of Arabic and
Persian literature, such as Arberry and Nicholson. However,
it was no longer in the vanguard of English letters.

English literature from the end of the nineteenth century
to the present has become very difficult to comprehend.
Indeed, serious works are often only understood by the critic
or the intellectual elite. There is no longer accessibility, for
the most part, to the depths of much of modern literature,
with the result that the unschooled often keep their distance.
In addition to the difficulty of modern works, the period is
marked by pessimism and cynicism. Such a negative attitude
when couched in a sparse, ideolectic style sets up a train of
associations which would hardly recommend itself to a
religious text. It may be safely said that all major religions
offer teachings which provide a positive approach to life and
assert the dignity and worth of humanity. A style of English
that might have been more modern in Shoghi Effendi's time
may not have been appealing to the target readers, owing
to is bleak associations. Perhaps Shoghi Effendi chose his
archaic style of English not only because it elicited reverence
on the part of the reader but because it was far removed
from modern trends and the negativity and futility of modern thought. In this sense, such a choice would lend itself to
Shoghi Effendi's goal of providing a lasting and enduring
translation.

Although a feature of modern literature is obscurity, the style of language Shoghi Effendi uses also poses difficulties of a different kind, that of employing archaic words that are not always understood and a style of English which, though reverent, is not in common use. These challenges, however, can be readily rectified by use of reference works and an attempt by the uninitiated reader to become accustomed to the style.

The register or voice Shoghi Effendi uses is a high one geared towards a fairly literate person. One might query why such a position was taken, especially in light of modern trends in translating the Bible, for example, in such a way that it can be easily understood by ordinary people, who in many societies may not be very well read. Shoghi Effendi's wife addresses this question:

> Shoghi Effendi chose, to the best of his great ability, the right vehicle for his thought and it made no difference to him whether the average person was going to know the word he used or not. After all, what one does not know one can find out. Although he had such a brilliant command of language he frequently reinforced his knowledge by certainty through looking up the word he planned to use in Webster's big dictionary . . . Not infrequently his choice would be the third or fourth usage of the word, sometimes bordering on the archaic, but it was the exact word that conveyed his meaning and so he used it.[158]

Here Rúḥíyyih Khánum is not just referring to Shoghi Effendi's translations but also to his own works in which he uses a very complex structural style and employs words which are used infrequently in daily conversation. Many readers of Shoghi Effendi comment that they need a dictionary to read his writing, and even well-educated people state that reference works are useful when perusing his works and translations. Of interest here, too, is the comment about his use of words in their third or fourth meaning. Even though

Shoghi Effendi used a conservative, obviously biblical style, his desire for acceptability did not include lowering literary standards in order to achieve this objective.

It is clear from this that Shoghi Effendi desired his readers to improve themselves, to rise to a higher level of literacy. He encouraged people to uplift themselves in all ways – his overall desire was that Bahá'ís achieve excellence in all things, including their use of language.

Shoghi Effendi used several techniques to achieve the elevated tone of the Hidden Words that identifies it as scripture. For example, words referring to the Deity or His Messengers are capitalized, here illustrated by the Prologue:

HE IS THE GLORY OF GLORIES

1 This is that which hath descended from the realm of
    glory,
2 uttered by the tongue of power and might, and revealed
3 unto the Prophets of old. We have taken the inner
    essence
4 thereof and clothed it in the garment of brevity,
    as a token
5 of grace unto the righteous, that they may stand faithful
6 unto the Covenant of God, may fulfil in their lives
    His trust,
7 and in the realm of spirit obtain the gem of
    Divine virtue.

'Prophets' (line 3), referring to the Messengers throughout the ages, is capitalized. The word 'God' (line 6) would usually be capitalized as a spelling convention in English but the capitalization of 'His' (line 6) and 'Divine' (line 7) lends the text a reverent and elevated tone. This effect can be seen again in Hidden Word Arabic 4:

O SON OF MAN!
1 I loved thy creation, hence I created thee. Wherefore,
2 do thou love Me, that I may name thy name
3 and fill thy soul with the spirit of life.

In this Hidden Word, 'Me' (line 2) is capitalized. 'Me' refers to God as the source of the revelation uttered by His messenger, Bahá'u'lláh. So, it would seem, two voices are included in the 'Me'. A reading of the text will show that this policy of capitalization is followed throughout.

Another technique which elevates the text can be discerned from these same passages, namely, the use of the archaic form of verbs and personal and possessive pronouns. Thus we see in the Prologue (line 1) 'hath descended' for the 'has descended' of modern usage. Again in Hidden Word Arabic 4 (line 2) the archaic, informal possessive pronoun 'thy' replaces the modern 'your', and the personal pronoun 'thou' is used for 'you'. These archaic words were used in the King James Bible. Here they biblicize the text and therefore elevate it. This device, too, is consistent throughout the translation and seems intended to convey the idea that the text is scripture and to elicit the appropriate attitude in the reader.

Another device used to elevate the language of the translation is inversion, which also gives emphasis to the statement and is frequently used in the Bible; this stylistic element imparts authority to the text, as in Hidden Word Arabic 23:

O SON OF THE SUPREME!
1 To the eternal I call thee, yet thou dost seek that
2 which perisheth. What hath made thee turn away
3 from Our desire and seek thine own?

The more usual sequence in line 1 would be 'I call thee to the eternal'. The inversion of the word order here is in harmony with an archaized biblical style and adds emphasis and authority to the passage.

The major norm of elevation is augmented by subordinate norms, just as was the norm of interpretation. In the above examples are three such subordinate norms. The first is 'capitalization', which can be stated as the policy 'capitalize nouns and personal and possessive pronouns which refer to the Deity'. The Prologue illustrates the use of capitalization. The second subordinate norm is found in Hidden Word Arabic 4: the use of archaic words to elevate the text, which I call the subordinate norm of 'archaisms', or, stated as a policy, 'use archaisms as in a biblical style'. The third example of subordinate norms is the use of 'inversion', which can also be put in command form: 'use inversion for effect and emphasis'. These subordinate norms exemplify how a major norm is propped up, so to speak, or carried by the subordinate norms.

The overlapping of the major and subordinate norms is a characteristic that will become increasingly clear as the discussion proceeds. Now that we have looked at two of the major norms, interpretation and elevation, instances can be cited where they function simultaneously in the production of the translation. Hidden Word Arabic 2, above, provides a good example of this phenomenon. Lines 8 and 9 read as follows: 'Verily justice is My gift to thee and the sign of My loving-kindness.' The word 'verily' functions in more than one capacity. It elevates the tone of the language in that it is archaic and a particularly 'biblical' word. It is an emphatic word meaning 'truly' which imparts a sense of authority in the text. Further, it is an addition to the text – this word is not in the original Arabic. As a policy the subordinate norm of 'addition' is to 'add to the text any elements not implicit in the original that are necessary'. Shoghi Effendi clearly added this word to carry an emphatic tone as part of his interpretation. Thus this subordinate norm of addition functions under both the major norms of elevation and interpretation at the same time. This illustration indicates how structurally complicated is the functioning of the major and subordinate norms, as will become more evident in the following pages.

The Major Norm of Beautification

The major norm of 'beautification' can be stated as a policy: 'beautify the English text'. Shoghi Effendi sought to create beauty in his translation of the Hidden Words as well as in his other endeavours, as can be seen in his landscaping, interior design and architectural projects. Beauty is a thread that runs through all his work and it would be odd if he did not seek to attain it in his translations. Rúḥíyyih Khánum tells us:

> His joy in words was one of his strongest personal character-istics, whether he wrote in English – the language he had given his heart to – or in the mixture of Persian and Arabic he used in his general letters to the East. Although he was so simple in his personal taste he had an innate love of richness which is manifest in the way he arranged and decorated various Bahá'í Holy Places, in the style of the Shrine of the Báb, in his preferences in architecture, and in his choice and combination of words.[159]

As his wife says, in his personal life Shoghi Effendi was very simple, but everything pertaining to or associated with the Bahá'í Faith was infused by him with beauty. Of course, everyone's standards of beauty differ. Shoghi Effendi's tastes were quite classical and conservative and in keeping with what is accepted as beautiful in Western and Middle Eastern civilization, and that trend towards conservatism is reflected in his choice of an antedated style of English traditionally considered beautiful in the English literary polysystem in which to render his translation of the Hidden Words. Rúḥíyyih Khánum describes Shoghi Effendi's thoughts about translating the beauty in the works of Bahá'u'lláh's writings into English:

> He . . . said he believed a few of the highly mystical and poetical writings of Bahá'u'lláh could never be translated as they would become so exotic and flowery that the original beauty and meaning would be completely lost and convey a wrong impression. Once . . . Shoghi Effendi said to me

that I now knew enough Persian to understand the original
and he read a paragraph of one of Bahá'u'lláh's Tablets and
said, 'How can one translate that into English?' For about
two hours we tried, that is he tried and I feebly followed
him. When I would suggest a sentence, which did convey
the meaning, Shoghi Effendi said, 'Ah, but that is not
translation! You cannot change and leave out words in the
original and just put what you think it means in English.'
He pointed out that a translator must be absolutely faithful
to his original text and that in some cases this meant that
what came out in another language was ugly and even
meaningless. As Bahá'u'lláh is always sublimely beautiful in
His words this could not be done. In the end he gave it up
and said he did not think it could ever be properly translated into English, and this passage was far from being one
of the more abstruse and mystical works of Bahá'u'lláh.[160]

Thus for Shoghi Effendi beauty in language was not only
highly desirable but necessary. Since he was aware of what
might 'convey a wrong impression', we can deduce that he
knew what would convey a right one. In other words, he
knew what was acceptable in the literary target system and
purposely chose a style of English that would find acceptance. He also knew that in English literature florid elaboration is not looked upon as the positive attribute it is in Arabic
literature: the norms of the English literary polysystem
generally preclude exotic and flowery translations. On the
other hand, more ornateness was acceptable for translations
of Near Eastern literature. Even so, and despite Shoghi
Effendi's use of a Victorian style of English, his sense of
propriety precluded over-ornateness in his translations. For
Shoghi Effendi, for a translation to be faithful, the beauty of
the original must be maintained. According to him, beauty
is an element for which there must be equivalence in the
target language or there can be no translation. Further, we
see that meaning must also be retained. So here we have

what might be stated as the transposition of both content (meaning) and form (beauty). We shall see that the major norms of interpretation and beautification appear side by side in Shoghi Effendi's translation of the Hidden Words.

Beautification of the text is also in keeping with the overriding objectives discussed above. As we have noted, an interpretation of the Bahá'í writings must include restructuring the beauty of the original or, in Shoghi Effendi's estimate, a translation is not possible. Thus beauty is a necessary component of dynamic equivalence and a translation that keeps the message intact but distorts the beauty of the original is not a faithful translation. In this sense, the overriding goal of 'to interpret the Bahá'í writings' is served by this major norm. In addition, a beautiful rendition will be more inspirational and better suited to devotional purposes, which also helps to spread the religion, since the believers will be sustained and inspired and attract others. As for providing a lasting translation that does not have to be periodically revised, a beautiful rendition will usually satisfy its readers, who will not then request new translations on the grounds of loveliness. In the past people expected a certain beautiful style of English in the Bible. In recent years this has changed and some translations, for example, emphasize comprehension, often at the cost of style and readability. Notwithstanding this modern development, Shoghi Effendi wanted to provide translations which would be recognized as scripture and stylistically acceptable. It is likely that for these reasons he wished to retain the element of beauty in his translation of the Hidden Words. It should also be remembered that he made several revisions of the text, working with it until he was satisfied that it was as beautiful as he could make it.

Let us now see how Shoghi Effendi employed the major norm of beautification, using Hidden Word Arabic 21 as an example:

٢١ ‎ ‎ *(يَا ٱبْنَ ٱلْبَشَرِ)*

قَدَّرْتُ لَكَ مِنَ ٱلشَّجَرِ ٱلْأَبْهَى ٱلْفَوَاكِهَ
ٱلْأَصْفَى كَيْفَ أَعْرَضْتَ عَنْهُ وَ رَضِيتَ
بِٱلَّذِي هُوَ أَدْنَى فَٱرْجِعْ إِلَى مَا هُوَ خَيْرٌ لَّكَ
فِي ٱلْأُفُقِ ٱلْأَعْلَى

O SON OF MAN!
1 Upon the tree of effulgent glory I have hung for
2 thee the choicest fruits, wherefore hast thou
3 turned away and contented thyself with that which
4 is less good? Return then unto that which is better
5 for thee in the realm on high.

A more literal translation of the first line might be 'I have ordained for thee from the tree of glory the choicest fruits'. However, Shoghi Effendi uses the word 'hung' for the Arabic قدرت (lit. 'ordain, decree'), thus choosing a fuller metaphor. In fact, in an earlier translation he did use 'ordain', later changing it to 'hung', which provides a lovelier tone and image. It is a norm in English to have complete tropes in which the thought is filled out and not merely suggested. In the English literary system the word 'ordain' in this context is not as satisfying as 'hung', as fruit usually hangs from trees. In this example the subordinate norm 'completion of a trope' originates from the major norm of beautification.

Another example of beautification is found in Hidden Word Arabic 13:

١٣ ٭(يَا ٱبْنَ ٱلرُّوحِ)٭

خَلَقْتُكَ غَنِيًّا كَيْفَ تُفْقِرُ وَ صَنَعْتُكَ

عَزِيزًا بِمَ تَسْتَذِلُّ وَمِنْ جَوْهَرِ الْعِلْمِ أَظْهَرْتُكَ

لِمَ تَسْتَعْلِمُ عَنْ دُونِى وَ مِنْ طِينِ

الْحُبِّ عَجَنْتُكَ كَيْفَ تَشْتَغِلُ بِغَيْرِى

فَارْجِعِ الْبَصَرَ إِلَيْكَ لِتَجِدَنِى فِيكَ قَائِمًا

قَادِرًا مُقْتَدِرًا قَيُّومًا

O SON OF SPIRIT!

1 I created thee rich, why dost thou bring thyself
2 down to poverty? Noble I made thee, wherewith
3 dost thou abase thyself? Out of the essence
4 of knowledge I gave thee being, why seekest
5 thou enlightenment from anyone beside Me?
6 Out of the clay of love I moulded thee, how dost
7 thou busy thyself with another? Turn thy sight
8 unto thyself, that thou mayest find Me standing
9 within thee, mighty, powerful and self-subsisting.

In line 6 is another use of the subordinate norm of completion of a trope in order to beautify a text. The words
'moulded you' for عجنتك (lit. 'kneaded you') in the Arabic
completes the metaphor since we associate clay with being
moulded into a form, not kneaded. Although the thought
is maintained, the words 'moulded you' read much more
smoothly and round out the metaphor.

In lines 8 and 9 the Arabic word فيك reads 'within thee'
rather than 'standing within thee'. This translation is a sign
of Shoghi Effendi's craftsmanship. The Hidden Word ends
with four attributes of God: قائماً قادراً مقتدراً قيوماً . In
English these could be read literally as 'the eternal, the
powerful, the powerful, the self-existent'. The Arabic word

قائما , which translates as 'eternal', comes from a verb that means 'to stand' (something that continues to stand or endure is eternal). Shoghi Effendi incorporates the sense of 'standing' from this into the phrase 'standing within you'. This leaves three attributes which are translated as 'mighty', 'powerful' and 'self-subsisting'. Whereas a string of four attributes might read in English like a catalogue rather than an inspirational statement, the list of three flows easily. Neither is the sense lost, as the concept of 'eternal' is maintained in the phrase 'standing within you', a state that, presumably, will not cease if one follows the injunction to 'turn thy sight unto thyself'.

In beautifying this line the subordinate norm of variation, which can be stated as 'do not use the same word in proximity in the text', is employed. In the string of four attributes there are two that mean 'powerful': قادراً and مقتدراً . Shoghi Effendi translates these as 'mighty' and 'powerful'. The thought remains intact but the line in English is more elegant.

The major norm of beautification overlaps with the norms of interpretation and elevation. As well as the norm of beautification, the norm of interpretation is employed in line 6 of this Hidden Word: the words 'moulded you' are an interpretation and are aesthetically affected. The subordinate norm of 'completing a trope' is also employed in both instances.

Looking back to Hidden Word Arabic 2 (line 1), we find another example of the simultaneous functioning of two major norms. When discussing the major norm of interpretation, we analyzed the phrase عندي 'in my sight'. Shoghi Effendi's interpretation of this phrase not only clarifies the meaning but is also far more pleasing. The phrase 'in my sight' is more aesthetically acceptable than the more literal versions of Shoghi Effendi's translation of the line 'The best beloved of all things in My sight is Justice':

* The best beloved all things I have is Justice.

* With me the best beloved of all things is Justice.

* Justice is the best beloved of all things with me.

* The best beloved of all things I possess is Justice.

* Justice is the best beloved of all things I possess.

All of these possibilities diminish the translation and are clumsy and unlovely. While there are surely many other versions of this line which could be considered, Shoghi Effendi's translation maintains equivalence by not sacrificing the beauty of the original.

These examples show that the overlapping of major norms is not unusual, as can also be observed from a perusal of the Norm Chart in chapter 7. Norms often overlap and exert their influence in the evolution of the rendition. Other instances of the overlapping of major and subordinate norms are illustrated in the following discussion of the major norm of 'euphonization'.

The Major Norm of Euphonization

The major norm of 'euphonization', which can be stated as 'euphonize the English text', is the last major norm isolated in Shoghi Effendi's translation of the Hidden Words. When euphony overlays a text, it is almost always very deliberately added by the writer and may follow particular rules within the target literary polysystem. As noted previously, Bahá'u'lláh's Arabic Hidden Words is permeated with music, so to speak, as it is written in the rhymed prose style of *saj'* and uses such devices as rhyme, non-structured metre, alliteration, consonance and assonance, all of which, when chanted or recited, create a certain music. Although the work is not poetry, it elicits the same response in the listener as poetry might do.

Since euphony is an important component of the Hidden Words in the Arabic, it follows that Shoghi Effendi exerted efforts to retain it in his English translation. Just as it was necessary to recreate beauty, the euphony had to be preserved as far as possible. Another consideration was probably the purposes the translation would serve orally in liturgical situations. Scriptures of all the major religions are not simply read silently but are very likely to be read aloud and heard by others. After all, literacy on any scale is a development of the twentieth century and even today there are many people who cannot read. Throughout the centuries, then, and even today, scripture is more often heard than read. The reading of scripture out loud often takes place in structured situations, such as in a church or in group study or devotions, with the literate person, often a member of the clergy, reading. Nida comments on this:

> The priority of the heard form of language over the purely written form is particularly important for translations of the Bible. In the first place, the Holy Scriptures are often used liturgically, and this means that many more people will hear the Scriptures read than will read them for themselves. Second, the Scriptures are often read aloud to groups as a means of group instruction . . . Last, the Scriptures are employed increasingly in such media as radio and television, which means that the oral form must be fully intelligible if the audience is to comprehend.[161]

Although Nida is speaking about Bible translating, his remarks can equally apply to translations of any of the world's scriptures. The Hidden Words is considered scripture by Bahá'ís around the world and in many of the places where Bahá'ís live there is widespread illiteracy. The Bahá'í scriptures are read aloud frequently, both in areas of illiteracy and as part of many Bahá'í devotional activities in general. Even where English is not used, Shoghi Effendi's English translation of the Hidden Words is used as a source text for translations into other languages and the musicality of his translations is transferred into these other languages.

Most gatherings of Bahá'ís include the oral reading of Bahá'u'lláh's writings. Many Bahá'ís also read prayers aloud in private. Among Eastern Bahá'ís, those of Persian and Arabic background, the writings and prayers are chanted or recited in the original tongues, a custom stretching back to the recitation of the Qur'án. So significant a feature of Bahá'í life is the recitation of the writings that for this reason alone Shoghi Effendi would surely have considered the preservation of the euphonic character of the Hidden Words indispensable.

Further, Shoghi Effendi may well have foreseen the role that the broadcast media would play in the future. When he translated the Hidden Words in the 1920s the radio was already in widespread use. He may well have realized that it would play an increasingly important role in mass communications and that religious programming would form a part of it. The scripture read over the radio needs to be pleasing to the ear or it will not draw an audience. At present there are several Bahá'í radio stations around the world which broadcast Bahá'í scriptures, sometimes in their English translation and more often in other languages translated from Shoghi Effendi's renditions. If Shoghi Effendi's translation of the Hidden Words was not so suited to be spoken aloud, its appropriateness for this purpose would be greatly diminished.

It is interesting to consider the effect of Shoghi Effendi's upbringing on the euphony of his translations. As we have seen, Shoghi Effendi was from an early age exposed to and taught the art of chanting the Persian and Arabic Bahá'í texts. By all accounts he chanted very beautifully. His wife provides an insight into how he composed his translations and other literary works:

> From the beginning of my life with the Guardian until the end, I was almost always present when he translated or wrote his books, long letters and cables in English. There was nothing unusual in this; he liked to have someone in

the room on these occasions to listen to what he was writing. His method of composition was new and fascinating to me. He wrote out loud, speaking the words as he put them down. I think this habit in English was carried over from Persian; good Persian and Arabic composition not only can be but should be chanted. One remembers the Báb revealing the *Qayyúmu'l-Asma'* out loud, and Bahá'u'lláh revealing His Tablets in the same way. This was the Guardian's custom in English as well as in Persian . . .[162]

It is probably the case that Shoghi Effendi translated the Hidden Words in the same way, speaking the words out loud, trying them out to see if the euphony of the Arabic and Persian was kept intact insofar as English would allow.

The production of a euphonic translation of the Hidden Words fulfils several of the overriding goals discussed earlier. A text in which one feels the rhythm and pulse of the words is appropriate for devotional purposes and will better inspire and sustain the believers, which in turn helps to spread the religion. The element of euphony also helps create a stylistically acceptable translation and one, therefore, that is more enduring.

Let us now look at how Shoghi Effendi used the norm of euphonization in his translation of the Hidden Words.

Euphonization is a constant throughout the text of the Hidden Words, so much so that to cite every example of it would be to overburden the reader. A few examples from the first three Arabic Hidden Words will demonstrate the point.

Shoghi Effendi uses several techniques to euphonize his translation, alliteration being a favourite, as his wife points out: 'He was very fond of the device of alliteration, much used in oriental languages but now no longer so common in English.'[163] In Hidden Word Arabic 1 we find the line 'Possess a pure, kindly and radiant heart, that thine may be a sovereignty ancient, imperishable and everlasting'. The subordinate norm of 'alliteration' can be stated as a policy: 'use alliteration where appropriate to euphonize the text.' In this verse there is repetition of the initial 's' sound in the address 'O Son of Spirit' and in 'sovereignty'; it also appears in 'possess' and in 'everlasting'. Other examples are the initial 'p' in the phrase 'Possess a pure' and the initial 'th' sound in 'that thine'. In this same line there is alliteration in the repetition of the 'r' sound in 'radiant' and 'heart', 'sovereignty' and 'imperishable'. There is also the repetition of the 'sh' sound in 'ancient' and 'imperishable'. Thus there is not only alliteration of one consonant but of several in the same words, which reinforces the line's poetic ring.

'Assonance' is another subordinate norm which can be stated as a policy: 'use assonance wherever appropriate to euphonize the text.' We can observe the repetition of the vowel sound of the long 'i' in 'kindly' and 'thine' in the same sentence. The subordinate norms of assonance and alliteration serve the major norm of euphonization in this Hidden Word, and by adding the dimension of assonance to alliteration there are even more layers of euphony imposed on the same words.

Now let us look again at Hidden Word Arabic 2 which is a good example of euphony employing rhyme and metre.

O SON OF SPIRIT!

1   The best beloved of all things in My sight is Justice;
2   turn not away therefrom if thou desirest Me
3   and neglect it not that I may confide in thee.
4   By its aid thou shalt see with thine own eyes and
5   not through the eyes of others, and shalt know of
6   thine own knowledge and not through the knowledge
7   of thy neighbour. Ponder this in thy heart;
8   how it behoveth thee to be. Verily justice is My
9   gift to thee and the sign of My loving-kindness. Set
10 it then before thine eyes.

In lines 2 and 3 we find the following: 'turn not away therefore if thou desirest *Me*, and neglect it not that I may confide in *thee*' (italics mine). The words 'Me' and 'thee' are a correlative end rhyme in each phrase and the lines have the same metre. The Arabic poetic prose form of *saj'* employs internal rhyme and a comparison of the two lines in English and Arabic shows that the rhyming word is in the very same place in both. The syllable count in the Arabic, read in the pausal form, is 13, while in English there are 12 syllables in the first clause and also in the second. This relationship is very close; not all examples are so closely allied. However, this illustration indicates the degree to which Shoghi Effendi sought to recreate the musicality of the original Arabic in his rendition, even to the extent of retaining the *saj'* form where possible.

Another example of this is also found in Hidden Word Arabic 2: 'By its aid thou shalt see with thine own eyes and not through the eyes of oth*ers*, and shalt know of thine own knowledge and not through the knowledge of thy neighb*our*' (italics mine). It should be mentioned that there are many rhyme possibilities in Arabic, whereas English has fewer words that rhyme, so an exact rhyme in English is more difficult to achieve. The rhyme Shoghi Effendi uses here at the end of each phrase is close but is not the exact match found in the Arabic. In Arabic rhymed prose each phrase has the same end rhyme and more or less the same metre. Here the metre in English is the same, with 18 syllables in each of the two phrases. In the Arabic, when read in the pausal form, the first phrase has 16 syllables and the second 19.

It is worth noting that there is a good deal of overlap in these examples of the subordinate norms of rhyme, metre, assonance and alliteration. There is also the same phenomenon over the overlapping of major norms. In Hidden Word Arabic 2, euphonization and elevation function simultaneously in line 2, and under the major norm of elevation is the subordinate norm of archaism, 'therefrom', 'thou' and 'desirest' being archaic words. In addition, in line 3 we find the major norm of interpretation overlapping with the norm of euphonization, since 'that I may confide in thee' is literally 'that you may be trustworthy with me'. We can say, then, that euphonization operates side by side with the other major and subordinate norms.

7

Norm Chart

The following chart looks at 18 Arabic Hidden Words and the Prologue line by line, pointing out instances of norms that are of particular note. In each line examined, major norms precede subordinate ones – a loose attempt to designate hierarchical relationships among the norms. Although the whole text is considered to be interpretation from the point of view of the Bahá'í Faith, this is not indicated in the following information, as only instances of interpretation of parts of the English Hidden Words that clarify the Arabic are included here. However, the word 'clarification' could have been used in place of 'interpretation' as a major norm. Even though it was not used in this way, the implication of 'clarification' as part of 'interpretation' must be kept in mind.

As for the norms of elevation and beautification, it can be argued, with justification, that these are employed in each and every Hidden Word; indeed, the chart is prepared on the assumption that this is so. To illustrate their presence in the Hidden Words, these norms are spelled out in detail in the analysis of the Prologue and of Hidden Words Arabic 1 to 4. For example, in each of these all of the archaisms are noted, as are all instances of capitalization of personal and possessive pronouns referring to the Deity. These devices for beautification and elevation are easily identified and, therefore, are not cited at each occurrence afterwards. For the remaining Hidden Words, only particular examples which illustrate the presence of these norms to a special degree are noted.

Euphonization, too, is a constant throughout the text of

the Hidden Words, although it is not structured with clearly defined rhyme and metre; however, the specialist can readily observe it functioning, while the non-specialist might intuit it. For the purposes of this chart, only a few particularized examples, in Hidden Words 1 to 3, are presented.

The same norm may function in more than one capacity, such as clarifying a concept while at the same time beautifying it, and so forth. The chart shows levels of meaning that have been observed but does not preclude the possibility of other levels of complexity and interrelationship.

Norm Chart

Prologue

HE IS THE GLORY OF GLORIES

1 This is that which hath descended from the realm of
  glory,
2 uttered by the tongue of power and might, and revealed
3 unto the Prophets of old. We have taken the inner
  essence
4 thereof and clothed it in the garment of brevity,
  as a token
5 of grace unto the righteous, that they may stand faithful
6 unto the Covenant of God, may fulfil in their lives
  His trust,
7 and in the realm of spirit obtain the gem of
  Divine virtue.

LINE	NORMS EMPLOYED (*in italics*)
INVOCATION	*Interpretation, beautification.* The Arabic reads هو البهى الابهى (lit. 'He is the Glorious, the Most Glorious').
1	*Elevation, archaisms*: 'hath'

1-2   *Interpretation*: نزل translates into 'descend' and 're-veal', each of which complements and completes the meaning. *Variation*: uses two different words for نزل , as above.

3   *Interpretation*: clarifies meaning by using 'inner essence' for 'intrinsic essence' or just 'essence'. *Elevation, capitalization*: capitalizes 'Prophets'.

4   *Elevation, archaisms*: 'thereof'

4-5   *Interpretation*: 'token of grace' for فضلًا

5   *Interpretation, beautification*: 'righteous' for احبار instead of 'learned man; non-Muslim religious authority; rabbi'.

5-6   *Interpretation, variation*: both وفى and ادّى 'fulfil' and other meanings. 'Stand faithful' clarifies what the 'righteous' do.

6   *Interpretation*: capitalizing 'Covenant of God'. بعهد الله indicates a specific concept in Bahá'í theology. Uses 'lives' for انفسهم , 'their own selves'. *Elevation, beautification*: Arabic does not use capitals as in English. 'His' is capitalized to refer to God.

7   *Omission*: The emphatic اَ has no counterpart in English. *Interpretation, beautification, emphasis*: uses verb instead of noun – 'obtain' is indicated in the Arabic by من الفائزين. *Elevation, capitalization*: capitalizes 'Divine'.

Hidden Word Arabic 1

O SON OF SPIRIT!
1 My first counsel is this: Possess a pure, kindly and
2 radiant heart, that thine may be a sovereignty ancient,
3 imperishable and everlasting.

LINE   NORMS EMPLOYED (*in italics*)

ADDRESS   *Elevation, beautification, archaism*: uses
            archaic invocation 'O' for يا .

1   *Interpretation*: makes a command – 'My first counsel
            is this' for فى اول القول . *Interpretation, beautification*:
            uses 'pure' for جيداً (lit. 'good, perfect, faultless') and
            'kindly' for حسناً (lit. 'good, beautiful').

2-3   *Beautification, omission, variation*: eliminates or com-
            bines دائماً and ازلاً (both lit. 'eternal') using one
            word, 'everlasting', for the two. Arabic prefers such
            repetitions, whereas English does not. *Inversion*:
            order is inverted: 'eternal, permanent, eternal,
            ancient'. *Euphonization, alliteration, assonance, rhythm*:
            repetition of 'sh', 's' and 'r' sounds as in 'Possess a
            pure, kindly and radiant heart' and in 'sovereignty
            ancient, imperishable and everlasting' and strong
            sense of rhythm, though no particular metre. Repeti-
            tion of 'i' sound in 'kindly' and 'thine' and 'e' sound
            in 'radiant', 'sovereignty' and 'be'.

Hidden Word Arabic 2

        O SON OF SPIRIT!
    1   The best beloved of all things in My sight is Justice;
    2   turn not away therefrom if thou desirest Me
    3   and neglect it not that I may confide in thee.
    4   By its aid thou shalt see with thine own eyes and
    5   not through the eyes of others, and shalt know of
    6   thine own knowledge and not through the knowledge
    7   of thy neighbour. Ponder this in thy heart;
    8   how it behoveth thee to be. Verily justice is My
    9   gift to thee and the sign of My loving-kindness. Set
   10   it then before thine eyes.

166

LINE NORMS EMPLOYED (*in italics*)

1   *Interpretation, beautification*: 'in My sight' for عندي (lit. 'I have; with me').

2   *Elevation, archaisms*: 'therefore', 'thou' and 'desirest' are archaic words.

2-3 *Euphonization, rhyme, metre*: 'Me' and 'thee' keep the same rhyme position as راغباً and أميناً. Rhyme and metre of Arabic and English matches.

3   *Interpretation*: 'that I may confide in thee' for the literal Arabic لتكون لى اميناً (lit. 'that you may be trustworthy with me').

4   *Beautification, omission*: الاشياء is eliminated, as is ها, the personal pronoun which refers back to it. *Interpretation, beautification, elevation*: 'By its aid' for the Arabic 'you will be given success (by God) in this (justice)'; 'eyes' for عين (lit. 'eye').

5   *Elevation, archaisms*: 'shalt' for 'shall'. *Beautification*: 'eyes of others' for عين العباد, (lit. 'eye of the servants').

4-8 *Euphonization, assonance, alliteration*: repetition of 'o', 'au' and 'u' sounds in 'thou', 'own', 'through', 'know', 'own knowledge', 'neighbour', 'how' and 'behoveth'. Repetition of 'n' sound in 'thine own', 'not', 'knowledge' and 'neighbour'.

6-7 *Interpretation, beautification*: 'through the knowledge of thy neighbour' for 'through the knowledge of anyone in the country' بمعرفة أحد فى البلاد.

7-10 *Elevation, archaisms*: 'thy', behoveth', 'thee' and 'thine' are archaic.

8   *Interpretation, emphasis*: puts 'justice is' for ذلك من (lit. 'this is'). *Interpretation, elevation, archaisms, emphasis, addition*: 'Verily' is not in the Arabic.

9   *Interpretation, beautification*: 'loving-kindness' for عناية (lit. 'concern, interest' and the specific connotation of 'divine solicitude').

167

10   *Emphasis, inversion*: 'then' is put in the middle of the sentence, which is more emphatic than at the beginning.

Hidden Word Arabic 3

O SON OF MAN!

1 Veiled in My immemorial being and in the ancient
2 eternity of My essence, I knew My love for thee;
3 therefore I created thee, have engraved on thee
4 Mine image and revealed to thee My beauty.

LINE   NORMS EMPLOYED (*in italics*)

1   *Interpretation, addition*: 'veiled' and 'ancient' are not in the Arabic. *Elevation*: 'My' has initial capital letter.

2   *Elevation:* 'My' has initial capital letter. *Elevation, archaisms:* 'thee'.

3   *Elevation, archaisms*: 'thee'. *Interpretation, elevation, archaisms, addition*: 'therefore' is not in the Arabic. *Interpretation, beautification*: 'engraved' used for القى (lit. 'throw; put').

4   *Elevation, archaisms, capitalization*: 'thee'; 'My' and 'Mine' have initial capital letters.

1-4   *Euphonization, alliteration, assonance*: repetition of 'v' sound in 'veiled', 'love', 'engraved' and 'revealed'; repetition of 'm' sound in 'My' and 'Mine'; repetition of 'th' sound in 'thee' and 'therefore'; repetition of long 'e' sound in 'immemorial being', 'eternity', 'My', 'thee', 'Mine', 'revealed' and 'beauty'.

Hidden Word Arabic 4

O SON OF MAN!

1 I loved thy creation, hence I created thee. Wherefore,
2 do thou love Me, that I may name thy name
3 and fill thy soul with the spirit of life.

LINE NORMS EMPLOYED (*in italics*)

2 *Interpretation*: 'name thy name' for اذكرك

3 *Interpretation, elevation, beautification, archaisms,*
   capitalization, completion of a trope: 'fill thy soul with
   the spirit of life' for وفى روح الحياة اثبتك (lit. 'in
   the soul, or spirit, of life make you steadfast');
   'thou', 'thy', 'Me'.

Hidden Word Arabic 5

O SON OF BEING!

1 Love Me, that I may love thee. If thou lovest Me
2 not, My love can in no wise reach thee. Know this,
3 O servant.

LINE NORMS EMPLOYED (*in italics*)

2 *Interpretation*: 'My love can in no wise reach thee' for
   لن احبك ابدأ (lit. 'I will not love you ever').

Hidden Word Arabic 7

O SON OF MAN!

1 If thou lovest Me, turn away from thyself; and if
2 thou seekest My pleasure, regard not thine own;
3 that thou mayest die in Me and I may eternally live
4 in thee.

LINE NORMS EMPLOYED (*in italics*)

2 *Beautification, variation*: uses 'thine own' instead of
repeating رضاء (lit. 'pleasure') as in the Arabic.

Hidden Word Arabic 8

O SON OF SPIRIT!
1 There is no peace for thee save by renouncing
2 thyself and turning unto Me; for it behoveth thee
3 to glory in My name, not in thine own; to put thy
4 trust in Me and not in thyself, since I desire to be
5 loved alone and above all that is.

LINE NORMS EMPLOYED (*in italics*)

4 *Beautification*: 'in Me' for على وجهى (lit. 'on my face');
'in thyself' for على وجهك (lit. 'on thy face').

Hidden Word Arabic 10

O SON OF UTTERANCE!
1 Thou art My stronghold; enter therein that
2 thou mayest abide in safety. My love is in thee,
3 know it, that thou mayest find Me near unto
4 thee.

LINE NORMS EMPLOYED (*in italics*)

3 *Beautification, omission*: منك is omitted.

170

Hidden Word Arabic 12

O SON OF BEING!

1 With the hands of power I made thee and with
2 the fingers of strength I created thee; and within
3 thee have I placed the essence of My light.
4 Be thou content with it and seek naught else,
5 for My work is perfect and My command is
6 binding. Question it not, nor have a doubt
7 thereof.

LINE   NORMS EMPLOYED (*in italics*)

4   *Interpretation*: 'seek naught else' for
           عن كل شىء (lit. 'from all things').

Hidden Word Arabic 13

O SON OF SPIRIT!

1 I created thee rich, why dost thou bring thyself
2 down to poverty? Noble I made thee, wherewith
3 dost thou abase thyself? Out of the essence
4 of knowledge I gave thee being, why seekest
5 thou enlightenment from anyone beside Me?
6 Out of the clay of love I moulded thee, how dost
7 thou busy thyself with another? Turn thy sight
8 unto thyself, that thou mayest find Me standing
9 within thee, mighty, powerful and self-subsisting.

LINE NORMS EMPLOYED (*in italics*)

6   *Beautification, completion of a trope*: 'moulded you' for
      عجنتك (lit. 'kneaded you'), which completes the
      metaphor.

8-9   *Interpretation, beautification, addition*: 'standing within
      thee' for فيك (lit. 'within you').

171

9   *Interpretation, beautification, omission*: eliminates قائماً
(lit. 'the Eternal [God]') as an attribute and incorporates it into 'standing within thee'. *Variation*: 'mighty,
powerful and self-subsisting' for قادراً مقتدراً قيوماً
(lit. 'powerful, powerful, self-existent'), giving two
different words for 'powerful'.

Hidden Word Arabic 14

O SON OF MAN!

1 Thou art My dominion and My dominion perisheth
2 not, wherefore fearest thou thy perishing?
3 Thou art My light and My light shall
4 never be extinguished, why dost thou dread
5 extinction? Thou art My glory and My glory
6 fadeth not; thou art My robe and My robe
7 shall never be outworn. Abide then in thy love
8 for Me, that thou mayest find Me in the realm
9 of glory.

LINE   NORMS EMPLOYED (*in italics*)

7   *Interpretation, beautification*: 'Abide' for استرح (lit. 'to
be calm; find rest').

8-9   *Interpretation, beautification*: 'realm of glory' for
الافق الاعلى (lit. 'highest horizon').

Hidden Word Arabic 21

O SON OF MAN!

1 Upon the tree of effulgent glory I have hung for
2 thee the choicest fruits, wherefore hast thou
3 turned away and contented thyself with that which
4 is less good? Return then unto that which is better
5 for thee in the realm on high.

LINE NORMS EMPLOYED (*in italics*)

1   *Beautification, completion of a trope*: 'hung' for قدرت
(Lit. 'ordain, decree'), which completes the metaphor.

4   *Emphasis, inversion*: 'then' after 'return' instead of
usual word order.

5   *Interpretation, beautification, variation*: 'realm on high'
for الافق الاعلى (lit. 'highest horizon'), a variation of
the same phrase in Hidden Word Arabic 14.

Hidden Word Arabic 22

O SON OF SPIRIT!
1 Noble have I created thee, yet thou hast abased
2 thyself. Rise then unto that for which thou wast
3 created.

LINE NORMS EMPLOYED (*in italics*)

1   *Beautification, elevation, emphasis, inversion*: 'Noble
have I created thee' rather than the usual word order,
'I have created thee noble'.

Hidden Word Arabic 23

O SON OF THE SUPREME!
1 To the eternal I call thee, yet thou dost seek that
2 which perisheth. What hath made thee turn away
3 from Our desire and seek thine own?

LINE   NORMS EMPLOYED (*in italics*)

ADDRESS *Interpretation, elevation, beautification, omission*: 'O Son of the Supreme' for يا ابن العماء .

1   *Elevation, beautification, inversion*: 'To the eternal I call thee' instead of the usual word order 'I call thee to the eternal'.

Hidden Word Arabic 24

O SON OF MAN!
1 Transgress not thy limits, nor claim that which
2 beseemeth thee not. Prostrate thyself before the
3 countenance of thy God, the Lord of might and
4 power.

LINE NORMS EMPLOYED (*in italics*)

3   *Beautification, substitution*; 'thy God' for ربك (lit. 'thy Lord') and 'Lord' for ذى .

Hidden Word Arabic 48

O SON OF MAN!
1 For everything there is a sign. The sign of love
2 is fortitude under My decree and patience under
3 My trials.

LINE NORMS EMPLOYED (*in italics*)

1   *Elevation, beautification, inversion*: 'For everything there is a sign' instead of the usual word order 'there is a sign for everything'.

Hidden Word Arabic 49

O SON OF MAN!

1 The true lover yearneth for tribulation even as
2 doth the rebel for forgiveness and the sinful
3 for mercy.

LINE NORMS EMPLOYED (*in italics*)

2   *Elevation, beautification, addition*: 'doth' adds a verb.

Hidden Word Arabic 50

O SON OF MAN!

1 If adversity befall thee not in My path, how
2 canst thou walk in the ways of them that are
3 content with My pleasure? If trials afflict thee not
4 in thy longing to meet Me, how wilt thou attain
5 the light in thy love for My beauty?

LINE NORMS EMPLOYED (*in italics*)

4   *Beautification, substitution*: 'attain' for يصيبك (lit. 'befall you').

8

Conclusion

Having considered the norms used by Shoghi Effendi in his translation of the Hidden Words, we need now to ask a very important question: 'Is his a successful translation?' Toury suggests how we might begin to answer this:

> When one's purpose is the descriptive study of literary translations in their environment, the initial question is not whether a certain text *is* a translation (according to some preconceived criteria which are extrinsic to the system under study), but whether it is *regarded* as a translation from the intrinsic point of view of the target literary polysystem, i.e. according to its position within the polysystem.[164]

My analysis has been carried out within the framework of a descriptive study; the text would not have merited study if it were not considered a translation in the target literary polysystem. Among English-speaking Bahá'ís around the world it is considered a valid translation and a sacred text. It is found in many libraries and, because of its nonsectarian, universal appeal, is often given as a gift to those who are not Bahá'ís. However, the main audience is a Bahá'í one, and it is the attitude of the Bahá'ís that is germane here. Most Bahá'ís consider Shoghi Effendi's translation of the Hidden Words a definitive rendering of a very important scriptural work of Bahá'u'lláh. To this extent, then, the translation is successful.

However, this does not go far enough. Is it successful according to Shoghi Effendi's criteria for success? Does it fulfil the textual goals elucidated in this book? If we remember, those textual goals were to inspire, to imbue with spiritual feeling, to make enduring, to make grand, to make elegant and to make eloquent. These are intangibles, of course, and they are not easy to determine, except subjectively; nevertheless it would appear that these goals have been fulfilled in Shoghi Effendi's translation of the Hidden Words.

It is difficult to speak critically about intangibles that are only relevant to those who experience them. Nonetheless, in determining whether this translation is successful there is no alternative.

The Hidden Words is, perhaps, the most frequently quoted Bahá'í text and its verses are often memorized. It is very often turned to in times of difficulty and is used as a source of guidance. It also forms the basis of meditation and reflection for many Bahá'ís. We might conclude from this, therefore, that it is, indeed, an inspirational work, imbued with spiritual feeling.

I believe the goals 'to make grand', 'to make elegant' and 'to make eloquent' are also fulfilled by Shoghi Effendi's translation. The writing has a dignity, stateliness and sense of grandeur which is unmistakable. The translation has none of the excesses of Victorian English and has all of the best virtues that nineteenth-century English had to offer.

Most people, of course, do not speak about a work being elegant or eloquent or grand, as most people are not articulate on literary matters. They know what they like and know what they understand, but to determine such attributes as elegance, eloquence and grandeur is particularly difficult. I have used these terms to indicate what I feel is in the text. On the other hand, tastes differ and some might prefer a different type of translation. However, calls for different translations of the Hidden Words are hardly, if ever, heard among Bahá'ís so it must be said that in this area too the translation is successful.

In another dimension as well Shoghi Effendi's translation

of the Hidden Words has been successful: it is used for second-hand translation, that is, translation of a translation. All of Shoghi Effendi's translations of Bahá'í writings are used for this purpose. In 1986, the last date for which statistics are available, Bahá'í literature had been translated into 802 languages.[165] Almost all of these translations have been made from the English translations of Shoghi Effendi.

Further, Shoghi Effendi's translations, including the Hidden Words, are the stylistic standard for all translations by subsequent translators of the Bahá'í writings into English. His work is a model for future translators to emulate. Indeed, present-day translators of Bahá'í scripture not already translated by Shoghi Effendi look to his language, style, translation norms and techniques for guidance in their own work. 'Abdu'l-Bahá said that in the future translations of the Bahá'í writings would be made by committees. The Translation Committee at the Bahá'í World Centre in Haifa, Israel, follows the standard set by Shoghi Effendi very closely. In this area, too, the translation of Shoghi Effendi of the Hidden Words can be considered successful.

It is sometimes suggested by Bahá'ís that Shoghi Effendi's translations will never be superseded and it is certainly true that no future translations will carry the authoritative interpretation with which Shoghi Effendi's are endowed. However, Shoghi Effendi has not stated that his translations will be the final ones. In the introduction to his translation of the Kitáb-i-Íqán he says:

> This is one more attempt to introduce to the West, in language however inadequate, this book of unsurpassed pre-eminence among the writings of the Author of the Bahá'í Revelation. The hope is that it may assist others in their efforts to approach what must always be regarded as the unattainable goal – a befitting rendering of Bahá'u'lláh's matchless utterance.[166]

In the future when enough time has elapsed to alter the English literary polysystem and the English language, it may be that revision or retranslation of Shoghi Effendi's translations will take place. Nevertheless, such a future translation will be just that: a translation and only a translation. The translator will not have the same status as Shoghi Effendi and will not be able to give the translation an unquestionable interpretation, nor will it be consulted as authoritative in the same way that Shoghi Effendi's translations are by the Universal House of Justice, the supreme governing body of the Bahá'í Faith. The Universal House of Justice refers to the Bahá'í sacred works and to Shoghi Effendi's translations and other writings when legislating on matters pertaining to the Bahá'í world community, when answering questions and advising people on issues. It will not be able to rely on new translations in the same way. It is my view that even if the works Shoghi Effendi translated are open for re-translation, this will not happen in the foreseeable future. Thus the enduring quality of Shoghi Effendi's translation of the Hidden Words is assured and another measure of its success.

As indicated earlier, a translation usually enters a target literary polysystem in the non-canonized position. In other words, it is not at the centre of the polysystem but at its periphery. The Hidden Words is not considered canonical in the English literary system, although it has certainly found its niche in that system. As time goes by, more people will read the Hidden Words owing to the increase in the membership of the Bahá'í community. The fate of the Hidden Words is tied up with the fate of the religion from which it comes. Its future, then, will be determined by the position the Bahá'í Faith occupies in the English-speaking world. If English continues to grow as an auxiliary world language, as may well happen, more and more people might potentially become exposed to the Hidden Words. If the Bahá'í Faith continues to grow, as Bahá'ís envision it will, then the Hidden Words might move into the centre of the English literary polysystem. If so, then Shoghi Effendi's translation, since it is already conservative, could become a model of English scriptural prose and exert great influence on the

English language and its sacred literature. In other words, it would do what the Bible has done in the past. If this happens, its success as a translation will be assured for centuries.

Appendix 1

The Appointment of Shoghi Effendi as Guardian and Expounder of the Bahá'í Faith

The Will and Testament of 'Abdu'l-Bahá names Shoghi Effendi as the Guardian and Interpreter of the Bahá'í Faith after His death. The first part of this three-part document was penned when Shoghi Effendi was only a child of five or so. The Will was kept a well-guarded secret, owing to the potential danger to Shoghi Effendi's own person and to the budding religion from the intrigues of 'Abdu'l-Bahá's enemies, both from within and without the Faith. The Will was kept in 'Abdu'l-Bahá's safe until He passed away on 28 November 1921. His family found the Will, addressed to Shoghi Effendi, and opened it to see if 'Abdu'l-Bahá had left any instructions about His funeral.

At the time of 'Abdu'l-Bahá's death Shoghi Effendi was in England. He was immediately recalled to the Holy Land but the news so shocked him that he collapsed. His physical condition and the tying up of his affairs in England delayed his arrival in Haifa until 29 December. The Will and Testament of 'Abdu'l-Bahá was read aloud for the first time to nine men on 3 January 1922 but Shoghi Effendi was not well enough to attend the reading.

Shoghi Effendi calls the Will and Testament of 'Abdu'l-Bahá 'His greatest legacy to posterity' and 'the brightest emanation of His mind'.[167] The Will was written in three parts, penned at different times during the years 1901 to 1908 when 'Abdu'l-Bahá was in great danger of being executed by the Turkish officials. In it He makes provision for the protection and continuation of His father's nascent Faith by, among other things, appointing Shoghi Effendi as Guardian and Interpreter of the Bahá'í Faith;[168] establishing the procedure for electing the Universal House of Justice;[169] appointing Shoghi Effendi as 'its sacred head and the distinguished member for life';[170] enjoining Bahá'ís to be 'submissive to all monarchs that are just' and to show 'fidelity to every righteous king';[171] establishing a body of nine Hands of the Cause to be resident in the Holy Land to assist the Guardian[172] (this institution of outstanding Bahá'ís appointed for their distinguished service to the Faith was initiated by Bahá'u'lláh); giving responsibility for their future appointment to Shoghi Effendi;[173] making it incumbent on Shoghi Effendi 'to appoint in his own life-time him that shall become his successor, that differences may not arise after his passing' and requiring his successor to be one of Shoghi Effendi's male lineal descendants or another male member of the family;[174] and warning the Bahá'ís to be ever vigilant against those who have broken the Covenant (those disaffected Bahá'ís who dispute the line of succession and are cast out; hence, their designation as 'Covenant-breakers') and seek to usurp authority.[175]

Shoghi Effendi is appointed by name in Parts One and Three as Guardian and Expounder. The following passage is from Part One:

> O my loving friends! After the passing away of this wronged one, it is incumbent upon . . . the loved ones of the Abhá Beauty to turn unto Shoghi Effendi – the youthful branch branched from the two hallowed and sacred Lote-Trees and the fruit grown from the union of the two offshoots of the Tree of Holiness, – as he is the sign of God, the chosen branch, the Guardian of the Cause of God, he unto whom all . . . must turn. He is the Interpreter of the Word of God and after him will succeed the first-born of his lineal descendents . . . The mighty stronghold shall remain im-

pregnable and safe through obedience to him who is the Guardian of the Cause of God . . . should the first-born of the Guardian of the Cause of God . . . not inherit of the spiritual within him (the Guardian of the Cause of God) and his glorious lineage not be matched with a goodly character, then must he, (the Guardian of the Cause of God) choose another branch [male member of the family] to succeed him.[176]

From this there can be no doubt whatsoever that Shoghi Effendi was intended as 'Abdu'l-Bahá's successor. He is called the 'Guardian of the Cause of God' and the 'Interpreter of the Word of God'. Obedience and loyalty to both the Guardian and the Universal House of Justice are enjoined on believers in no uncertain terms. The Universal House of Justice was first elected in 1963, five and half years after the death of Shoghi Effendi. The function of the Universal House of Justice is legislative whereas the Guardian's role is executive.

Shoghi Effendi was the first and only Guardian. He had no children and none of the male members of the family were faithful Bahá'ís. Thus Shoghi Effendi was unable to appoint a successor and he was the last interpreter of the Bahá'í writings. However, the institution of the Guardianship is considered by Bahá'ís to continue to exist in that Shoghi Effendi's interpretations and expositions are still binding upon Bahá'ís and will continue to be so. The vast body of Shoghi Effendi's works in the form of letters, books and translations is referred to by individual Bahá'ís and by Bahá'í institutions at the local, national and international level. Thus while the Universal House of Justice is authorized to enact laws not explicitly revealed in the writings of Bahá'u'lláh, before enacting legislation or declining to do so, or answering questions from Bahá'ís, it first refers to the Bahá'í writings on the subject and any commentary by Shoghi Effendi.

At the very end of Part Three of His Will and Testament,

'Abdu'l-Bahá, in a gesture of love for his grandson, again calls him by name:

> O ye the faithful loved ones of 'Abdu'l-Bahá! It is incumbent upon you to take the greatest care of Shoghi Effendi . . . that no dust of despondency and sorrow may stain his radiant nature, that day by day he may wax greater in happiness, in joy and spirituality, and may grow to become even as a fruitful tree.
>
> For he is, after 'Abdu'l-Bahá, the Guardian of the Cause of God . . . and the beloved of the Lord must obey him and turn unto him . . . Beware lest anyone falsely interpret these words, and like unto them that have broken the Covenant after the Day of Ascension (of Bahá'u'lláh) advance a pretext, raise the standard of revolt, wax stubborn and open wide the door of false interpretation. To none is given the right to put forth his own opinion or express his particular conviction. All must seek guidance and turn unto the Centre of the Cause and the House of Justice. And he that turneth unto whatsoever else is indeed in grievous error.
>
> The Glory of Glories rest upon you![177]

Hence Shoghi Effendi is held in high esteem by Bahá'ís everywhere and his translations considered authoritative.

Appendix 2

Shoghi Effendi's Accomplishments

A brief overview of Shoghi Effendi's accomplishments is presented here to give a fuller picture of his life work. So vast are the achievements of Shoghi Effendi, it is difficult to understand how he accomplished so much in the 36 years of his Guardianship. In her biography of him, Shoghi Effendi's wife quotes her own diaries:

> Temperamentally Shoghi Effendi is a doer, a builder, an organizer, and loathes abstractions! . . . He is the most extraordinarily uni-directional person I have ever seen . . . He is like something travelling at high speed in one direction, which gives him almost infinite driving power. His persistence is irresistible; there is no dissipation of his forces. He only wants one thing, he wants it passionately, immediately, completely, perfectly. The Temple built – or a flight of steps here in the garden. He descends on it like a hurricane and never lets up until it is done. He drives ahead. It is extraordinary.[178]

It was this single-mindedness and perseverance coupled with, among other things, a gift for organization and administration which enabled Shoghi Effendi to accomplish so much: 'A born administrator, with a brain and temperament that were invariably orderly and tidy, Shoghi Effendi set about organizing the affairs of the Faith in a highly systematic manner'.[179] Rúḥíyyih Khánum comments that 'his genius for organization' was 'one of his strongest characteristics'.[180]

This 'genius for organization' enabled Shoghi Effendi to take the provisions of the Will and Testament of 'Abdu'l-

Bahá, the Kitáb-i-Aqdas, Bahá'u'lláh's Book of the Covenant and other Tablets, and forge the beginnings of the Administrative Order of the Bahá'í Faith which Bahá'u'lláh envisaged. This Order was to be worldwide in compass, composed of local assemblies, elected by local believers; national assemblies, elected by delegates; and the Universal House of Justice, elected by the National Spiritual Assemblies of the world. When 'Abdu'l-Bahá passed away, there were only a handful of local spiritual assemblies in existence, no national spiritual assemblies and no Universal House of Justice. Shoghi Effendi was the master-engineer who took the blueprints provided by the writings of Bahá'u'lláh and 'Abdu'l-Bahá and built the administrative edifice from the ground up:

> . . . there were few Spiritual Assemblies in the world, and only one national body [the Baha'i Temple Unity] functioning in a very rudimentary manner . . . the Great Administrator . . . with a world-encompassing vision, set about his task. Patiently, persistently, painstakingly, Shoghi Effendi reared strong national bodies. He brought into being the International Bahá'í Council – the embryonic Universal House of Justice.[181]

By 1953 there were twelve national spiritual assemblies; in 1957 Shoghi Effendi announced that there were over a thousand local spiritual assemblies in the world.[182] When the Universal House of Justice was elected in 1963 at the conclusion of a Ten Year International Teaching Plan which Shoghi Effendi had inaugurated, there were 56 national spiritual assemblies.

Shoghi Effendi galvanized the Bahá'ís of the world to prosecute both regional and worldwide plans to develop and expand the Bahá'í Faith. Through his constant guidance, counsel, education, encouragement and careful monitoring of events through correspondence and cables, Shoghi Effendi saw the Bahá'í Faith grow from a obscure religion based largely in the Middle East with a few hundred believers in North America and Europe, to a global religion established by the time of his death in virtually every country of the world.

This, however, was not his only work. While he was engaged in the development, expansion and consolidation of the Bahá'í Faith, he oversaw a multitude of other tasks:

> . . . the emancipation of the Cause from Islam in Egypt, formally and forcibly pronounced a non-Muḥammadan independent faith by the ecclesiastical authorities there, which in its turn greatly strengthened the Bahá'í claim to official recognition as a new and independent world religion in other lands, including the United States; the tremendous increase of Bahá'í properties the world over, including not only six National Headquarters but innumerable local headquarters, meeting halls, guesthouses and even burial grounds . . . the purchase, in the land of Bahá'u-'lláh's birth, of most of the sacred and historic sites associated with the rise of the Faith there, as well as an extensive and beautiful property destined to be the site of the future Bahá'í Temple in that country; the increase in the number of Bahá'í summer schools . . . the truly remarkable output of Bahá'í literature . . . the legal incorporation of . . . national and local Bahá'í Assemblies in countries all over the world . . .[183]

In addition, Shoghi Effendi had Bahá'í marriage recognized as legal in many countries; had Bahá'í properties exempted from taxes; established and maintained friendly relations with the British Mandate and later the State of Israel and had Bahá'í properties there recognized as Shrines and Holy Places; had himself recognized as Head of an independent world religion; steadily built up the prestige of the Faith in Israel and around the world; championed the human rights of the Bahá'í Faith's adherents in Iran where Bahá'ís were still subject to outbreaks of fanaticism and hostility leading to imprisonment and death; inaugurated a worldwide campaign culminating at the League of Nations to protest the seizure of the House of Bahá'u'lláh in Baghdad, a place of Bahá'í pilgrimage; strove to reacquire other properties wrested away by enemies of the Faith and Covenant-breakers; oversaw the building of the House of Worship in Wilmette, Illinois, a 50-year project begun in the days of 'Abdu'l-Bahá; mounted two large-scale architectural projects, the superstructure of the Shrine of the Báb and the International Archives Building, both on the slopes of Mount Carmel at the Bahá'í World Centre; designed and personally laid out the large formal gardens at the Bahá'í World Centre and at the Shrine of Bahá'u'lláh in Acre; directed and encouraged the translation of the Bahá'í writings into the world's languages, work which he often financed himself; and directed the orderly publication and dissemination of Bahá'í literature around the globe. At the same time he carried on a voluminous correspondence with individual Bahá'ís and Bahá'í institutions around the world, wrote a history of the Bábí and Bahá'í Faiths and undertook the translations of the writings of Bahá'u'lláh, one of which is the subject of this book.

Appendix 3

Translations of the Hidden Words

Prologue

Kheiralla

He is El-behi-ul-abha. This is that which descended from the Majestic Might through the Tongue of Power and Strength upon the prophets of the past. We have taken its essences and clothed them with the garment of Brevity, as a favor upon the divines that they may fulfill the Covenant of God and be able to perform in themselves what He entrusted to them; that they may win, by the essence of piety, in the land of the Spirit, the Victory.

Fareed

HE IS EL-BAHA-EL-ABHA!

He is the Glory of
The Most Glorious!

(1) This is that which descended from the Source of Majesty, through the Tongue of Power and Strength upon the prophets of the past. We have taken its essences and clothed them with the garment of brevity, as a favor to the beloved, that they may fulfil the Covenant of God; that they may perform in themselves that which He has entrusted to them, and attain the victory by virtue of devotion in the land of the Spirit:

Stannard

HE IS EL-BAHIO-EL-ABHA!

He is The Glory of
The Most Glorious!

This is that which was revealed through the tongue of Power and Might upon the Prophets of the past; from the Source of the Most High.*

* *Ar. 'Gaberout'. (of Sublimity). This term frequently used implies might, power, sovereignty, of divine order.*

Shoghi Effendi 1923

He is the Glory of Glories

This is that which hath descended from the Realm of Glory, uttered by the Tongue of Power and Might and revealed unto the Messengers of old, the quintessence whereof We have taken and arrayed in the garment of brevity, as a token of grace unto the righteous that they may stand faithful unto the Covenant of the Lord, that they may fulfil in their lives His Trust, and may in the Realm of the Spirit obtain for themselves the priceless gem of Divine Virtue.

Shoghi Effendi 1929

HE IS THE GLORY OF GLORIES

This is that which hath descended from the realm of glory, uttered by the tongue of power and might, and revealed unto the Prophets of old. We have taken the inner essence thereof and clothed it in the garment of brevity, as a token of grace unto the righteous, that they may stand faithful unto the Covenant of God, may fulfil in their lives His trust, and in the realm of spirit obtain the gem of Divine virtue.

Arabic 1

Kheiralla

O Son of Spirit! The first utterance is, Possess a good, pure and enlightened heart, that thou mayest possess a continual, everlasting, unceasing and ancient Kingdom.

Fareed

(2) O SON OF SPIRIT!
The first counsel is this: Possess a good, a pure, an enlightened heart, that thou mayest possess a Kingdom eternal, immortal, ancient, and without end.

Stannard

1. O SON OF SPIRIT.
The first of Counsels is this, possess a good, pure and shining (enlightened) heart that thou mayest possess an everlasting, ancient and eternal Kingdom.

Shoghi Effendi 1923

(1) O SON OF SPIRIT!
My first counsel is this: Possess a pure, kindly and radiant heart, that thine may be a sovereignty, heavenly, ancient, imperishable and everlasting.

Shoghi Effendi 1929

1. O SON OF SPIRIT!
My first counsel is this: Possess a pure, kindly and radiant heart, that thine may be a sovereignty ancient, imperishable and everlasting.

Arabic 2

Kheiralla

O Son of Spirit! The best of all to Me is justice. Desire thou not to cast it away, if thou desirest Me, and neglect it not, that thou mayest be faithful to Me, for by it, thou wouldst succeed to see all the things with thine own eye and not by the eye of the creatures, and know them by thine own knowledge and not by the knowledge of any in the world. Think over this – how thou oughtest to be. Justice is one of My Gifts to thee and one of My Cares over thee, therefore put it before thine eyes continually.

Fareed

(3) O SON OF SPIRIT!
Justice is loved above all. Neglect it not, if thou desirest Me. By it thou wilt be strengthened to perceive things with thine own eyes and not by the eyes of men, to know them by thine own knowledge and not by the knowledge of any in the world. Meditate on this – how thou oughtest to be. Justice is of My Bounty to thee and of My Providence over thee; therefore, keep it ever before thy sight.

Stannard

O SON OF SPIRIT.
Justice* (or Equity) must be loved above all things, forsake it not if thou desirest My Will. Neither neglect it if thou wouldst be faithful. By it thou shalt be strengthened (or confirmed) to perceive things with thine own eyes and not with the eyes of others, to know things by thine own knowledge and not by that of any other in the world. Meditate on this, and reflect that this counsel is from My Grace and bounty to thee, so keep it ever in thy sight.

* (Ar. 'Insaf).

194

Shoghi Effendi 1923

2. O SON OF SPIRIT!

Of all things Justice is the best beloved in My Sight; turn not away therefrom if thou desirest Me, and neglect it not that I may confide My Trust to thee. By its aid thou shalt see with thine own eyes and not with the eyes of others, and shalt know by thy own understanding and not by the understanding of thy neighbour. Ponder this in thy heart; how it behoveth thee to be. In truth Justice is My gift to thee and the sign of My loving-kindness unto Thee. Set it then before thine eyes.

Shoghi Effendi 1929

2. O SON OF SPIRIT!

The best beloved of all things in My sight is Justice; turn not away therefrom if thou desirest Me, and neglect it not that I may confide in thee. By its aid thou shalt see with thine own eyes and not through the eyes of others, and shalt know of thine own knowledge and not through the knowledge of thy neighbour. Ponder this in thy heart; how it behoveth thee to be. Verily justice is My gift to thee and the sign of My loving-kindness. Set it then before thine eyes.

Arabic 3

Kheiralla

O Son of Man! Thou hast been in My Ancient Identity and in My Everlasting Being. I knew My love in thee, therefore I created thee and laid upon thee the garment of My likeness and manifested to thee My Beauty.

Fareed

(4) O SON OF MAN!
In My Ancient Entity and in My Eternal Being, was I hidden. I knew My love in thee, therefore I created thee; upon thee I laid My Image, and to thee revealed My Beauty.

Stannard

O SON OF MAN.
In My ancient and eternal Being I knew My love in thee therefore did I create thee and laid on thee My Image, and revealed to thee My Beauty.

Shoghi Effendi 1923

3. O SON OF MAN!
Veiled in My immemorial Being and in the ancient eternity of My Self, I felt My Love for thee; hence, I created thee, have graven on thee the Image of My Likeness and revealed to thy sight the beauty of My Countenance.

Shoghi Effendi 1929

3. O SON OF MAN!
Veiled in My immemorial being and in the ancient eternity of My essence, I knew My love for thee; therefore I created thee, have engraved on thee Mine image and revealed to thee My beauty.

Arabic 4

Kheiralla

O Son of Man I loved thy creation; for this I created thee. Therefore love Me, that I may mention thee and in the Spirit of Life, confirm thee.

Fareed

(5) O SON OF MAN!
I loved thy creation, therefore I created thee. Wherefore love Me,
that I may acknowledge thee and in the Spirit of Life confirm
thee.

Stannard

O SON OF MAN.
I Loved thy creation, therefore I created thee; wherefore love thou
Me that I may remember** thee and in the spirit of Life confirm
thee.

** (*Lit. 'mention'*).

Shoghi Effendi 1923

4. O SON OF MAN!
I loved thy creation, hence I created thee. Wherefore, do thou love
Me, that I may name thy name and fill thy soul with the Spirit of
Life.

Shoghi Effendi 1929

4. O SON OF MAN!
I loved thy creation, hence I created thee. Wherefore, do thou love
Me, that I may name thy name and fill thy soul with the spirit of
life.

Arabic 5

Kheiralla

O Son of Existence! Love Me, that I may love thee. If thou wouldst
not love Me, I can never love thee. Know that, O Servant!

Fareed

(6) O SON OF EXISTENCE!
Love Me, that I may love thee. If thou lovest Me not, My love can never reach thee. Know this, O Servant!

Stannard

O SON OF BEING.
Love Me that I may love thee, if thou lovest Me not, My love can never reach thee. Know this O servant

Shoghi Effendi 1923

5. O SON OF BEING!
Love Me, that I may love thee. If thou lovest Me not, My love can in no wise reach thee. Know this, O servant.

Shoghi Effendi 1929

5. O SON OF BEING!
Love Me, that I may love thee. If thou lovest Me not, My love can in no wise reach thee. Know this, O servant.

Arabic 6

Kheiralla

O Son of Existence! Thy paradise is My Love and thy heaven is My nearness! Therefore be impatient to enter into it. This is what was ordained to thee in Our Highest Kingdom and Supreme Majesty.

Fareed

(7) O SON OF EXISTENCE
Thy paradise is My Love; thy heaven is My Nearness: Therefore
enter thou and tarry not. This was ordained for thee from Our
Supreme Kingdom and Exalted Majesty.

Stannard

O SON OF EXISTENCE!
In My love is thy happiness, (Riswan) and in communion with Me
is thy paradise. Enter therein and tarry not. Thus is it ordained
for thee in our Supreme Kingdom (Melakoot) and from our
Exalted Realm. (Gaberout).

Shoghi Effendi 1923

6. O SON OF BEING!
Thy Eden is My Love, and reunion with Me thy heavenly home.
Enter there-in and tarry not. This is that which hath been destined
for thee in Our Kingdom above and Our Exalted Paradise.

Shoghi Effendi 1929

6. O SON OF BEING!
Thy Paradise is My love; thy heavenly home, reunion with Me.
Enter therein and tarry not. This is that which hath been destined
for thee in Our kingdom above and Our exalted Dominion.

Arabic 7

Kheiralla

O Son of Humanity! If thou desirest Myself, desire not thyself, and
if thou wishest My Pleasure, shut thine eye from thy pleasure, that
thou mayest die in Me, and I live in thee.

Fareed

(8) O SON OF HUMANITY!
If thou lovest Me, turn away from thyself; if My Will thou seekest, regard not thine own, that thou mayest die in Me, and I live in thee.

Stannard

O SON OF HUMANITY.
If thou lovest Me, turn away from thy own pleasure. If My Will thou seekest regard not thine own, so shalt thou die in Me and I live in thee!

Shoghi Effendi 1923

7. O SON OF MAN!
If thou lovest Me, turn away from thyself; and if thou seekest My Pleasure, regard not thy own; that thou mayest utterly die in Me and I eternally live in thee.

Shoghi Effendi 1929

7. O SON OF MAN!
If thou lovest Me, turn away from thyself; and if thou seekest My pleasure, regard not thine own; that thou mayest die in Me and I may eternally live in thee.

Arabic 8

Kheiralla

O Son of Spirit! No peace was ordained to thee save by cutting thyself from thyself and depending upon Me, for thy glory must be in My Name and not in thy name; and thy dependence upon

My Face and not upon thy face; I alone deserve to be beloved above all things.

Fareed

(9) O SON OF SPIRIT!
No peace is ordained for thee save by departing from thyself and coming to Me. Verily, thy glory should be in My Name, not in thy name; thy trust upon My Countenance, not upon thine own; for I will to be loved above all that is.

Stannard

O SON OF SPIRIT.
No peace is ordained for thee save by departing from thy self and coming unto Me. Verily thy glory should be in My Name and not in thine own, Thy trust in My Countenance and not in thine own, for I desire to be loved alone and above all that is.

Shoghi Effendi 1923

8. O SON OF SPIRIT!
There is no rest for thee except if thou dost renounce thyself and turn unto Me; for it behoveth thee to glory in My Name and not in thine, and to put thy trust in Me and not in thyself. For I desire to be loved alone and above all else.

Shoghi Effendi 1929

8. O SON OF SPIRIT!
There is no peace for thee save by renouncing thyself and turning unto Me; for it behoveth thee to glory in My name, not in thine own; to put thy trust in Me and not in thyself, since I desire to be loved alone and above all that is.

Arabic 9

Kheiralla

O Son of Existence! My Love is My Fort: Whosoever enters it, is protected and safe, and he who rejects it, leads himself stray and perishes.

Fareed

(10) O SON OF EXISTENCE!
My Love is My Fortress. Who enters therein is rescued and safe; whoever turns away from it is led astray and perishes.

Stannard

O SON OF EXISTENCE.
My fortress (for thee) is My love. Who so enters therein is sheltered and safe but who so turns away from it is led astray, and perishes.

Shoghi Effendi 1923

9. O SON OF BEING!
My Love is My Stronghold; he that entereth therein shall be safe and secure, and he that turneth away shall surely stray and perish.

Shoghi Effendi 1929

9. O SON OF BEING!
My love is My stronghold; he that entereth therein is safe and secure, and he that turneth away shall surely stray and perish.

Arabic 10

Kheiralla

O Son of Beyan! My Fort thou art; therefore enter into it, that thou mayest be saved. My love is in thee; therefore know it from thyself that thou mayest find Me near.

Fareed

(11) O SON OF PERCEPTION! (*Beyan*)
My Fort thou art: Enter thou in that thou mayest be safe. My Love is in thee: Seek, and thou wilt find Me near.

Stannard

O SON OF ELOQUENCE! (BEYAN)*
My fortress thou art, enter within that thou mayest be secure. My love is within thee, know (realise) this so thou shalt find Me near.

* (*Exposition. Dialectic, etc.*).

Shoghi Effendi 1923

10. O SON OF UTTERANCE!
Thou art My Stronghold; enter therein that thou mayest abide in safety. My Love is in thee, know it that thou mayest find Me nigh unto thee.

Shoghi Effendi 1929

10. O SON OF UTTERANCE!
Thou art My stronghold; enter therein that thou mayest abide in safety. My love is in thee, know it, that thou mayest find Me near unto thee.

Arabic 11

Kheiralla

O Son of Existence! My Bowl thou art, and My Light is in thee:
Therefore be enlightened by it, and seek not any beside Me, for
I have created thee rich and abundantly bestowed Grace upon
thee.

Fareed

(12) *O Son of Existence!*
My lamp thou art, and My Light is in thee: Therefore be illumined
by it, and seek no one but Me, for I have created thee rich and
upon thee have I showered abundant grace.

Stannard

O SON OF BEING.
My lamp thou art and My light is within thee be therefore illumined by it. Seek no one but Me, for I created thee rich and upon
thee have I showered abundant Grace.

Shoghi Effendi 1923

11. O SON OF BEING!

Thou art My Lamp and My Light is in thee. Get thee light therefore and seek none other than Me, for I have created thee rich
and have bountifully favoured thee.

Shoghi Effendi 1929

11. O SON OF BEING!
Thou art My lamp and My light is in thee. Get thou from it thy
radiance and seek none other than Me. For I have created thee
rich and have bountifully shed My favour upon thee.

Arabic 12

Kheiralla

O Son of Existence! By the Hands of Power I made thee and by the Fingers of Strength I created thee and deposited in thee the essence of My Light: Therefore depend upon it and not upon anything else, for My Action is perfect and My Command must take its effect. Do not disbelieve this, and have no doubt in it.

Fareed

(13) O SON OF EXISTENCE!
By the Hands of Power I have made thee, and by the Fingers of Strength have I created thee. I have placed in thee the essence of My Light: Therefore depend upon it, and upon nothing else, for My Action is perfect and My Command has effect. Doubt this not, and have no uncertainty therein.

Stannard

O SON OF EXISTENCE!
With the hands of Power I made thee, and by the fingers of strength I created thee. In thee I placed the Essence of My Light see that thou depend on it and on nought else, for My creation is perfect and My Command cometh to its effect. Doubt this not and have thou no uncertainty.

Shoghi Effendi 1923

12. O SON OF BEING!
With the Hands of Power I made thee and with the Fingers of Might I created thee; and in thee have I placed the essence of My Light. Be thou content with it above all else, for My Work is perfect and My Command is binding. Question it not and have thou no doubt.

205

Shoghi Effendi 1929

12. O SON OF BEING!
With the hands of power I made thee and with the fingers of strength I created thee; and within thee have I placed the essence of My light. Be thou content with it and seek naught else, for My work is perfect and My command is binding. Question it not, nor have a doubt thereof.

Arabic 13

Kheiralla

O Son of Spirit! I have created thee rich: How is it that thou art poor? And made thee mighty: How is it that thou art low? From the essence of knowledge I manifested thee: How is it that thou seekest someone beside Me? And from the clay of love I kneaded thee: How is it that thou occupiest thyself with someone else? Turn thy sight to thyself, that thou mayest find Me standing in thee, Powerful, Mighty and Supreme.

Fareed

(14) O SON OF SPIRIT!
I have created thee rich: Why dost thou make thyself poor? Noble have I made thee: Why dost thou degrade thyself? Of the essence of Knowledge have I manifested thee: Why searchest thou for another than Me? From the clay of Love I have kneaded thee: Why seekest thou another? Turn thy sight unto thyself, that thou mayest find Me standing within thee, Powerful, Mighty and Supreme.

Stannard

O SON OF SPIRIT.
I created thee rich, why makest thou thyself poor? Noble I made thee why dost thou degrade thyself? Out of the essence of Knowledge I manifested thee, why seekest thou knowledge from another than Me?

From the clay of love I kneaded thee, why art thou occupied with another? Turn thy sight into thyself that Thou mayest find Me standing within thee, all powerful, mighty and supreme (lit. self existent).

Shoghi Effendi 1923

13. O SON OF SPIRIT!

I have created thee rich, wherefore impoverish thyself? Noble I made thee, wherewith does thou abase thyself? Out of the essence of Knowledge I manifested thee, why seekest thou any one beside Me? Of the clay of Love I moulded thee, why dost thou busy thyself with another? Turn thine eyes unto thyself, that in thee thou mayest find Me abiding, Mighty, Powerful and Self-Subsisting.

Shoghi Effendi 1929

13. O SON OF SPIRIT!

I created thee rich, why dost thou bring thyself down to poverty? Noble I made thee, wherewith dost thou abase thyself? Out of the essence of knowledge I gave thee being, why seekest thou enlightenment from anyone beside Me? Out of the clay of love I moulded thee, how dost thou busy thyself with another? Turn thy sight unto thyself, that thou mayest find Me standing within thee, mighty, powerful and self-subsisting.

Arabic 14

Kheiralla

O Son of Man! Thou art My Possession and My Possession will never be destroyed: How is it that thou art afraid of thy destruction? Thou art My Light and My Light will never be extinguished: How is it that thou dreadest extinction? Thou art My Splendor, and My Splendor never will be darkened: Thou are My Garment, and My Garment will never be worn out: Therefore dwell in thy love to Me that thou mayest find Me in the Highest Horizon.

Fareed

(15) O SON OF MAN!

Thou art My Possession, and My Possession shall never be destroyed: Why art thou in fear of thy destruction? Thou art My Light, and My Light shall never become extinct: Why dost thou dread extinction? Thou art My Glory (*Baha*), and My Glory shall not be veiled: Thou art My Garment, and My Garment shall never be outworn. Therefore abide in thy love to Me, that thou mayest find Me in the Highest Horizon.

Stannard

O SON OF MAN.

Thou art My possession and My possession can never be destroyed. Why art thou in fear of destruction? Thou art of My Light and My Light shall never be extinguished. Why dost thou dread extinction! Thou art of My Glory (or Beauty), and My Glory can never be veiled, thou art My Garment and My Garment shall never be outworn. Therefore abide in thy love for Me, that thou mayest find Me in the Supreme horizon! (or Concourse).

Shoghi Effendi 1923

14. O SON OF MAN

Thou art My Dominion and My Dominion perisheth not, wherefore fearest thou perishing? Thou art My Light and My Light shall never be extinguished, why dreadest thou extinction? Thou art My Glory and My Glory fadeth not; thou art My Robe and My Robe shall never be destroyed. Abide then in thy love for Me, that thou mayest find Me in the Realm of Glory.

Shoghi Effendi 1929

14. O SON OF MAN!

Thou art My dominion and My dominion perisheth not, wherefore fearest thou thy perishing? Thou art My light and My light shall never be extinguished, why dost thou dread extinction? Thou art My glory and My glory fadeth not; thou art My robe and My robe shall never be outworn. Abide then in thy love for Me, that thou mayest find Me in the realm of glory.

Arabic 15

Kheiralla

O Son of Beyan! Face all (the people) by My Face and cast away anyone beside Me, for My Authority is everlasting and will never cease; My Kingdom is a continual one and has no end, and if thou seekest some one beside Me, thou shalt not find, even if thou searchest the universe for ever and ever.

Fareed

(16) O SON OF PERCEPTION! (*Beyan*)
Look thou to My Face, and turn from all save Me, for My Authority is eternal and shall never cease, My Kingdom is lasting and shall not be overthrown. If thou seekest another than Me, yea, if thou searchest the universe forevermore, yet shall thy search be vain.

Stannard

O SON OF ELOQUENCE (BEYAN)
Look thou to My Face, and turn from all save Me, for My Dominion is eternal and shall never cease. My Kingdom is an everlasting Kingdom and shall never pass away. Wouldst thou seek another than Me, yea, wert thou to search the universe throughout eternity, yet would thy search be in vain [sic]

Shoghi Effendi 1923

15. O SON OF UTTERANCE!
Turn thy face unto Mine and renounce all else but Me; for My Sovereignty endureth and My Dominion perisheth not. Wert thou to seek another than Me, surely thou shalt fail, shouldst thou search the universe for evermore.

Shoghi Effendi 1929

15. O SON OF UTTERANCE!
Turn thy face unto Mine and renounce all save Me; for My sovereignty endureth and My dominion perisheth not. If thou seekest another than Me, yea, if thou searchest the universe for evermore, thy quest will be in vain.

Arabic 16

Kheiralla

O Son of Light! Forget all things beside Me, and be comforted by My Spirit. This is from the Essence of My Command: Therefore direct thyself to it.

Fareed

(17) O SON OF LIGHT!
Forget all else save Me, and be comforted by My Spirit. This is from the essence of My Command: therefore direct thyself to it.

Stannard

O SON OF LIGHT.
Forget all else save Me, and be comforted by My Spirit. This is from the essence of My Command therefore direct thyself to it.

Shoghi Effendi 1923

16. O SON OF LIGHT!
Forget all else but Me and commune with My Spirit. This is the essence of My Command, turn unto it.

Shoghi Effendi 1929

16. O SON OF LIGHT!
Forget all save Me and commune with My spirit. This is of the essence of My command, therefore turn unto it.

Arabic 17

Kheiralla

O Son of Man! Let thy satisfaction be in Myself and not in those who are inferior to Me, and seek not help from any beside Me, for nothing beside Me will ever satisfy thee.

Fareed

(18) O SON OF MAN!
Let thy satisfaction be in Me, rich above all else. Ask for no other helper than Me, for none but Me can ever satisfy thee.

Stannard

O SON OF MAN.
Let thy satisfaction in Me exclude all else (or every other desire). Ask for no other helper than Myself, for none beside Me can ever satisfy thee.

Shoghi Effendi 1923

17. O SON OF MAN!
Be thou content with My Self and seek no helper but Me, for none
but Me can ever suffice thee.

Shoghi Effendi 1929

17. O SON OF MAN!
Be thou content with Me and seek no other helper. For none but
Me can ever suffice thee.

Arabic 18

Kheiralla

O Son of Spirit! Ask thou not of Me that which thou dost not
desire for thyself. Then be contented with what We have ordained
for thy face, for that which We have ordained for thee, will benefit
thee – if thou art contented with it.

Fareed

(19) O SON OF SPIRIT!
Ask thou not of Me that which thou desirest not for thyself. Be
contented with what We have ordained for thy sake (*face*): This is
for thy good, if thou art content with it.

Stannard

O SON OF SPIRIT.
Ask not of Me that which we have not desired for thee; be content
with that which we have ordained for thy sake. This is for thy good
if thou wilt be content therewith.

Shoghi Effendi 1923

18. O SON OF SPIRIT!
Ask not of Me that which thou desirest not for thyself and be content with that which We have ordained for thee, for this is that which profiteth thee, if therewith thou doest content thyself.

Shoghi Effendi 1929

18. O SON OF SPIRIT!
Ask not of Me that which We desire not for thee, then be content with what We have ordained for thy sake, for this is that which profiteth thee, if therewith thou dost content thyself.

Arabic 19

Kheiralla

O Son of the Highest Appearance! I deposited in thee a Spirit from Me that thou might'st be My Lover: Why hast thou left Me and sought another lover?

Fareed

(20) O SON OF THE HIGHEST SIGHT!
I have placed within thee a spirit from Me, that thou mightest be My Lover: Why has thou forsaken Me and sought to love another?

Stannard

19. O CHILD OF SUPREME VISION.*
I have placed within thee a spirit from Myself, that thou mightest become My lover. Why has thou forsaken Me and sought to love another.

* *Appearance or Presentation.*

213

Shoghi Effendi 1923

19. O SON OF THE WONDROUS VISION!
I have breathed in thee a breath of My spirit, that thou mayest love
Me. Why hast thou forsaken Me and sought a beloved other than
Me?

Shoghi Effendi 1929

19. O SON OF THE WONDROUS VISION!
I have breathed within thee a breath of My own Spirit, that thou
mayest be My lover. Why hast thou forsaken Me and sought a
beloved other than Me?

Arabic 20

Kheiralla

O Son of Spirit! My Right to thee is great and cannot be forgotten;
My Favor upon thee is grand and cannot be hidden; My Love to
thee is existing and cannot be covered; My Light to thee is apparent and cannot be secluded.

Fareed

(21) O SON OF SPIRIT!
My Right to thee is great and cannot be denied. My Mercy for
thee is ample and cannot be ignored. My love in thee exists and
cannot be concealed. My Light to thee is manifest and cannot be
obscured.

Stannard

O SON OF SPIRIT.
My favor to thee is great and should not be denied. My bounty
towards thee is great and cannot be hidden. My love in thee exists

and cannot be concealed; My Light to thee is manifest and cannot be obscured.

Shoghi Effendi 1923

20. O SON OF SPIRIT!
Great is My Claim upon thee, it can not be forgotten. Abounding is My Grace unto thee, it can not be veiled. My Love is dwelling in thee, it cannot be concealed. Manifest is My Light unto thee, it cannot be hidden.

Shoghi Effendi 1929

20. O SON OF SPIRIT!
My claim on thee is great, it cannot be forgotten. My grace to thee is plenteous, it cannot be veiled. My love has made in thee its home, it cannot be concealed. My light is manifest to thee, it cannot be obscured.

Appendix 4

Major Writings of Shoghi Effendi

Books and book-length letters

1938 *The Advent of Divine Justice*

1941 *The Promised Day is Come*

1944 *God Passes By*

Translations

1923 *Prayer of Bahá'u'lláh; Prayers and Tablets of 'Abdu'l-Bahá*

1923 *Words of Wisdom, revealed by Bahá'u'lláh*

1923 'Tablet revealed by 'Abdu'l-Bahá to Dr Auguste Forel' 21 September 1921

1929 *The Hidden Words of Bahá'u'lláh*

1931 *Kitáb-i-Íqán* (The Book of Certitude), by Bahá'u'lláh

1933 *Tablets Revealed in Honour of the Greatest Holy Leaf*, by Bahá'u'lláh and 'Abdu'l-Bahá

1935 *Gleanings from the Writings of Bahá'u'lláh*

1938 *Prayers and Meditations by Bahá'u'lláh*

1941 *Epistle to the Son of the Wolf*, by Bahá'u'lláh

Bibliography

'Abdu'l-Bahá. *Tablets of Abdul-Baha Abbas*. New York: Bahá'í Publishing Committee, 1930.

— *A Traveller's Narrative Written to Illustrate the Episode of the Báb*. Trans. E. G. Browne. Cambridge: Cambridge University Press, 1891.

— *The Will and Testament of 'Abdu'l-Bahá*. Trans. Shoghi Effendi. Wilmette, Illinois: Bahá'í Publishing Committee, 1944.

al-Ahadith al-Qudsiyyia. Cairo: Majlis al-'Ala li al-shu'un al-Islamiyya, 1969.

Arberry, A. J. *Sufism: An Account of the Mystics of Islam*. London: George Allen and Unwin Ltd, 1956.

— trans. *Muslim Saints and Mystics: Episodes from 'the Tadhkirat al-Awliya' ('the Memorial of the Saints') by Farid al-Din Attar*. Chicago: The University of Chicago Press, 1966.

Arnold, Matthew. *The Poems of Matthew Arnold*. Kenneth Allott, ed. New York: Barnes and Noble, Inc., 1965.

The Bahá'í Centenary: 1844-1944. Wilmette, Illinois: Bahá'í Publishing Committee, 1944.

The Bahá'í Faith: Information Statistical and Comparative. Haifa, Israel: Bahá'í World Centre, n.d.

Bahá'í News, no. 107, April 1937.

The Bahá'í World, vol. 4. New York City: Bahá'í Publishing Committee, 1933.

Bahá'u'lláh. *Gleanings from the Writings of Bahá'u'lláh*. Trans. Shoghi Effendi. New York: Bahá'í Publishing Committee, 1935.

— *Hidden Words of Bahá'u'lláh*. Trans. Shoghi Effendi. New York City: Bahá'í Publishing Committee, 1924.

— *The Hidden Words of Bahá'u'lláh*. Trans. Shoghi Effendi. London: National Spiritual Assembly of the Bahá'ís of Great Britain and Northern Ireland, 1929.

— *The Hidden Words of Bahá'u'lláh*. Trans. Shoghi Effendi. New York: Bahá'í Publishing Committee, 1932.

— *The Hidden Words of Bahá'u'lláh*. Trans. Shoghi Effendi. New York: Bahá'í Publishing Committee, 1940.

— *The Hidden Words of Bahá'u'lláh*. Trans. Shoghi Effendi. Wilmette, Illinois: Bahá'í Publishing Committee, 1954.

— *Hidden Words From the Supreme Pen of Baha'u'llah*. Trans. Mrs J. Stannard. Cairo, 1921.

— *Hidden Words, Words of Wisdom and Communes: From 'The Supreme Pen' of Baha'u'llah*. Trans. Amin U. Fareed. Chicago: Bahá'í Publishing Society, 1905.

— *The Kitáb-i-Íqán: The Book of Certitude*. Trans. Shoghi Effendi. New York: Bahá'í Publishing Committee, 1931.

— *Prayers and Meditations by Bahá'u'lláh*. Trans. Shoghi Effendi. New York: Bahá'í Publishing Committee, 1938.

Balyuzi, H. M. *'Abdu'l-Bahá*. London: George Ronald, 1971.

Banani, Amin. 'The Writings of 'Abdu'l-Bahá'. *World Order*. Fall 1971.

— 'The Writings of 'Abdu'l-Bahá'. *The Bahá'í World*, vol. 15, pp. 781-4. Haifa: The Universal House of Justice.

Braun, Eunice. *A Reader's Guide*. Oxford: George Ronald, 1986.

Browne, E. G. *A Literary History of Persia: 1500-1924*. Cambridge: The University Press, 1969.

— *A Year Amongst the Persians*. Cambridge: Cambridge University Press, 1926.

Burton, Richard F., trans. *The Book of the Thousand Nights and a Night: A Plain and Literal Translation of the Arabian Nights Entertainments.* New York: The Heritage Press, 1885.

Catford, J. R. *A Linguistic Theory of Translation: An Essay in Applied Linguistics.* London: Oxford University Press, 1965.

Collins, Amelia. *A Tribute to Shoghi Effendi.* Wilmette, Illinois: Bahá'í Publishing Trust, n.d.

The Encyclopaedia of Islam. Leiden: E. J. Brill, 1971.

Evan-Zohar, Itamar. *Papers in Historical Poetics.* Tel Aviv: The Porter Institute for Poetics and Semiotics, 1978.

— 'Polysystem Theory'. *Poetics Today: Theory and Analysis of Literature and Communication,* vol. 1. Tel Aviv: The Porter Institute for Poetics and Semiotics, 1979-80.

— *Toward a Science of Translating with Special Reference to Principles and Procedures Involved in Bible Translating.* Leiden: E. J. Brill, 1964.

FitzGerald, Edward, trans. *Rubáiyát of Omar Khayyám.* No. 11, New York: St Martin's Press, 1983.

Gerhardt, Mia I. *The Art of Story-Telling: A Literary Study of the Thousand and One Nights.* Leiden: E. J. Brill, 1963.

Giachery, Ugo. *Shoghi Effendi: Recollections.* Oxford: George Ronald, 1974.

Goldziher, Ignaz. *Muslim Studies,* vol. 2. S. M. Stern, ed. Albany: State University of New York Press, 1971.

Grundy, Julia M. *Ten Days in the Light of 'Akká.* Wilmette, Illinois: Bahá'í Publishing Trust, 1979.

Hofman, David. Balyuzi Lecture, Association for Bahá'í Studies Conference, Ottawa, Canada, 1984.

— *George Townshend.* Oxford: George Ronald, 1983.

Kheiralla, Ibrahim George. *Beha'U'llah (The Glory of God).* Chicago: I. G. Kheiralla, Publisher, 1900.

Lang, Andrew, trans. *The Arabian Nights Entertainments*. London: Longmans, Green and Co., 1898.

Lewis, Frank. 'Towards a Literary Archeology of Bahá'u'lláh's *The Hidden Words*'. University of Chicago: Unpublished paper, 1985.

Lights of Guidance: A Bahá'í Reference File. Compiled by Helen Hornby. New Delhi: Bahá'í Publishing Trust, 2nd edn. 1988.

The Meaning of the Glorious Qur'án: Text and Explanatory Translation. Trans. Muhammad M. Pickthall. New York: Muslim World League, 1977.

Momen, Moojan. *Dr. J. E. Esslemont*. London: Bahá'í Publishing Trust, 1975.

al-Nawawi. *al-Arba'un*, no 14. n.d.

Nicholson, Reynold A. *The Mystics of Islam*. London: Routledge and Kegan Paul, 1979.

— trans. *Rumi: Poet and Mystic*. London: George Allen and Unwin Ltd.

Nida, Eugene A. and Jan de Ward. *From One Language to Another: Functional Equivalence in Bible Translating*. Nashville, Tennessee: Thomas Nelson, Inc., 1986.

Nida, Eugene A. and Charles R. Taber. *The Theory and Practice of Translation*. Leiden: E. J. Brill, 1974.

The Norton Anthology of English Literature, vol. 2. New York: W. W. Norton & Company, Inc., 1974.

Prendergast, W. J. *The Maqamat of Badi' al-Zaman al-Hamadhani*. Curzon Press, Ltd, 1973.

Rabbaní, Rúḥíyyih. *The Priceless Pearl*. London: Bahá'í Publishing Trust, 1969.

— *Twenty-Five Years of the Guardianship*. Wilmette, Illinois: Bahá'í Publishing Committee, 1948.

Sachedina, Abdulaziz. *Islamic Messianism*. Albany: State University of New York Press, 1981.

Shoghi Effendi. *God Passes By*. New York: Bahá'í Publishing Committee, 1938.

— *Unfolding Destiny*. London: Bahá'í Publishing Trust, 1981.

— *The World Order of Bahá'u'lláh*. New York: Bahá'í Publishing Committee, 1938.

The Six Year Plan: 1986-1992. Haifa: The Universal House of Justice, 1993.

Steiner, George. *After Babel: Aspects of Language and Translation*. New York: Oxford University Press, 1977.

Taherzadeh, Adib. *The Revelation of Bahá'u'lláh*, vol. 1. Oxford: George Ronald, 1974.

Toury, Gideon. *In Search of a Theory of Translation*. Jerusalem: Academic Press, 1980.

The Universal House of Justice, *The Seven Year Plan, 1979-1986, Statistical Report*. Haifa: Bahá'í World Centre.

Weinberg, Robert. *Ethel Jenner Rosenberg*. Oxford: George Ronald, 1995.

Whitmore, Bruce W. *The Dawning Place*. Wilmette, Illinois: Bahá'í Publishing Trust, 1984.

Yazdi, Ali M. *Blessings Beyond Measure*. Wilmette, Ill.: Bahá'í Publishing Trust, 1988.

References

1. Taherzadeh, *Revelation of Bahá'u'lláh*, vol. 1, pp. 126-7.
2. Toury, *In Search of a Theory of Translation*, p. 51.
3. Rabbani, *Priceless Pearl*, pp. 4-8.
4. ibid. p. 10.
5. 'Abdu'l-Bahá, first Tablet to Shoghi Effendi, Zia Baghdadi, trans. from Baghdadi's recollections, photographic copy of the original, 16 September 1932, Chicago, Illinois.
6. ibid.
7. ibid.
8. Rabbaní, *Priceless Pearl*, p. 9.
9. ibid. pp. 8-9.
10. ibid. p. 22.
11. Balyuzi, *'Abdu'l-Bahá*, p. 401.
12. ibid, pp. 96-7.
13. Rabbaní, *Priceless Pearl*, p. 9.
14. Letter from 'Alí Nakhjavání to the author, 7 November 1985.
15. ibid.
16. See, for example, Whitmore, *Dawning Place*, pp. 3-4.
17. *Bahá'í News*, no. 107, April 1937, p. 1.
18. ibid.
19. Rabbaní, *Priceless Pearl*, p. 13.
20. ibid. pp. 15-16.
21. ibid. p. 17.
22. Yazdi, *Blessing Beyond Measure*, pp. 49-50.
23. Rabbaní, *Priceless Pearl*, p. 18.
24. Yazdi, *Blessings Beyond Measure*, p. 51.
25. ibid. pp. 53-4.
26. Rabbaní, *Priceless Pearl*, p. 20.
27. Balyuzi, *'Abdu'l-Bahá*, pp. 400-1.
28. Yazdi, *Blessings Beyond Measure*, p. 54.
29. Rabbaní, *Priceless Pearl*, p. 25.
30. Yazdi, *Blessings Beyond Measure*, p. 61.

31. Rabbaní, *Priceless Pearl*, p. 12.
32. ibid. p. 30.
33. ibid.
34. ibid. p. 31.
35. ibid. p. 36.
36. Letter from John Jones, Archivist, Balliol College, 25 September 1985.
37. Yazdi, *Blessings Beyond Measure*, pp. 78-9.
38. ibid. pp. 81-2.
39. Rabbaní, *Priceless Pearl*, p. 37.
40. ibid.
41. Letter of 'Alí Nakhjavání, 7 November 1985.
42. ibid.
43. Amin Banani, 'The Writings of 'Abdu'l-Bahá', *World Order*, vol. 6, no. 1, Fall 1971, p. 67.
44. Letter of 'Alí Nakhjavání, 7 November 1985.
45. ibid.
46. ibid.
47. Quoted in Rabbaní, *Priceless Pearl*, p. 11.
48. ibid. pp. 15-16.
49. Balyuzi, *'Abdu'l-Bahá*, pp. 359-62.
50. Grundy, *Ten Days in the Light of 'Akká*, p. 84.
51. Letter of 'Alí Nakhjavání, 7 November 1985.
52. Rabbaní, *Priceless Pearl*, p. 37.
53. ibid. p. 225.
54. Shoghi Effendi, *God Passes By*, pp. 138-9.
55. Bahá'u'lláh, *Kitáb-i-Íqán*, American edition.
56. Rabbaní, *Priceless Pearl*, p. 214.
57. ibid. pp. 214-15.
58. ibid. p. 217.
59. ibid. p. 218.
60. Bahá'u'lláh, *Gleanings*, American edition.
61. Bahá'u'lláh, *Prayers and Meditations*, American edition.
62. Rabbaní, *Priceless Pearl*, p. 219.
63. Shoghi Effendi, *God Passes By*, pp. 219-20.
64. The Universal House of Justice, *The Seven Year Plan, 1979-1986, Statistical Report*, p. 28.
65. Rabbaní, *Priceless Pearl*, p. 220.
66. ibid. pp. 225-6.
67. Shoghi Effendi, *Unfolding Destiny*, pp. 209-10.

68. Rabbaní, *Priceless Pearl*, p. 209.
69. Letter from Shoghi Effendi to David Hofman, cited by David Hofman at the Association for Bahá'í Studies Hasan Balyuzi Memorial Lecture, Ottawa, Canada, 1984.
70. David Hofman, in the Association for Bahá'í Studies Hasan Balyuzi Memorial Lecture, Ottawa, Canada, 1984.
71. 'Abdu'l-Bahá, *Will and Testament*, 1971 American edition (based on the 1922 translation), p. 11.
72. Shoghi Effendi, *World Order of Bahá'u'lláh*, p. 148.
73. 'Abdu'l-Bahá, *Will and Testament*, American edition.
74. *Webster's New World Dictionary*.
75. Shoghi Effendi, *God Passes By*, pp. 139-40.
76. Taherzadeh, *Revelation of Bahá'u'lláh*, vol. 1, p. 71.
77. Bahá'u'lláh, *Hidden Words*, Prologue.
78. Shoghi Effendi, *God Passes By*, p. 140.
79. From a letter written on behalf of Shoghi Effendi to an individual Bahá'í 22 October 22 1949, cited in *Lights of Guidance*, no. 1633.
80. *The Meaning of the Glorious Qur'án*, p. xvi.
81. Lewis, *Towards a Literary Archeology of Bahá'u'lláh's Hidden Words*, p. 14.
82. Pickthall, *The Meanings of the Glorious Qur'án*, p. 739.
83. Banani, 'The Writings of 'Abdu'l-Bahá', *Bahá'í World*, vol. 15, p. 781.
84. Prendergast, *The Magámát*, p. 8.
85. Lewis, *Towards a Literary Archeology of Bahá'u'lláh's Hidden Words*, p. 17.
86. *The Meaning of the Glorious Qur'án*, p. 739.
87. Bahá'u'lláh, *Hidden Words*, Arabic 40.
88. *The Meaning of the Glorious Qur'án*, 109:1-6, p. 734-5.
89. Goldziher, *Muslim Studies*, vol. 2, p. 18.
90. Lewis, referring to al-Nawawi, *al-Arba'un*, no. 14, p. 10.
91. ibid. pp. 22-3.
92. *Encyclopedia of Islam*, vol. 3, p. 29.
93. Lewis, *al-Arba'un*, p. 24.
94. Cited in ibid. p. 25.
95. Cited in ibid.
96. See Nicholson, *The Mystics of Islam*.
97. Trans. Arberry, *Muslim Saints and Mystics*, pp. 1-3.
98. ibid. pp. 1-9.

99. Arberry, *Sufism*, pp. 113-14.
100. Taherzadeh, *Revelation of Bahá'u'lláh*, vol. 1, pp. 71-2.
101. Shoghi Effendi, *God Passes By*, p. 140.
102. Lewis, 'Towards a Literary Archeology of the Hidden Words', p. 21.
103. Cited in Lewis, p. 45.
104. 'Abdu'l-Bahá, *Traveller's Narrative*, p. 68.
105. ibid. pp. 122-6.
106. Browne, *Literary History of Persia*, vol. 4, pp. 311-12.
107. ibid. p. 423.
108. ibid. pp. 413-15.
109. Kheiralla, *Beha'U'llah*, p. 521.
110. From a letter written on behalf of Shoghi Effendi to an individual Bahá'í, 22 October 1949, cited in *Lights of Guidance*, no. 1633.
111. The *Union Catalog* lists *Hidden Words, Words of Wisdom, and Communes* published by the Bahai Publishing Society of Chicago as the first translation of the Hidden Words made by Shoghi Effendi. It also lists a book with the same title translated by Fareed as well as Fareed's 1905 translation entitled *Hidden Words, Words of Wisdom, and Communes from the Supreme Pen of Baha'u'llah*. In his *Bibliography of English-Language Works on the Bábí and Bahá'í Faiths 1844-1985*, p. 4, William Collins indicates that the first of these was published in 1905 and includes two pages at the end in which 'Abdu'l-Bahá answers questions about the Hidden Words. Thus Shoghi Effendi could not be the translator, as he would have been only eight years old at the time of its publication.
112. Letter from Muhammad Afnan, 13 June 1937.
113. Letter from Marzieh Gail, 3 December 1984.
114. Browne, *Year Amongst the Persians*, p. 635.
115. Browne, translating the Hidden Words in 'Abdu'l-Bahá, *A Traveller's Narrative*, p. 69.
116. *The Book of a Thousand Nights and a Night*, pp. 24-5.
117. *Arabian Nights Entertainments*, p. 122.
118. Arnold, *Poems of Matthew Arnold*, pp. 329-30.
119. Khayyám, *Rubáiyát*, no. 11.
120. Rúmí, *Rúmí: Poet and Mystic*, p. 31.
121. Rabbaní, *Priceless Pearl*, pp. 37-8.
122. *Norton Anthology of English Literature*, vol. 2, p. 895.

123. Rabbaní, *Priceless Pearl*, pp. 224-5.
124. Momen, Dr J. E. Esslemont, p. 2.
125. ibid. p. 9.
126. ibid. p. 31.
127. ibid. pp. 32-3.
128. *Bahá'í World*, vol. 4, p. 263.
129. ibid.
130. ibid.
131. Hofman, *George Townshend*, pp. 55.
132. Weinberg, *Ethel Jenner Rosenberg*, p. 64.
133. Hofman, *George Townshend*, p. 59.
134. ibid. p. 236.
135. ibid. pp. 250-1.
136. Cited in ibid. p. 318.
137. ibid. p. 241.
138. ibid. pp. 59, 77.
139. Weinberg, *Ethel Jenner Rosenberg*, p. 247.
140. Letter from Marzieh Gail, 3 December 1984.
141. Hofman, *George Townshend*, p. 81.
142. Catford, *Linguistic Theory of Translation*, p. 101.
143. ibid. p. 93.
144. Nida and Taber, *Theory and Practice of Translation*, p. vii.
145. Nida, *Toward a Science of Translating*, p. 165.
146. ibid. p. 167.
147. Even-Zohar, 'Polysystem Theory', *Poetics Today*, vol. 1, p. 288.
148. ibid. p. 290.
149. Even-Zohar, *Papers in Historical Poetics*, pp. 11-28.
150. Toury, *In Search of a Theory of Translation*, pp. 39, 43, 49-82.
151. ibid. p. 30.
152. ibid. pp. 52-3.
153. ibid. pp. 53-4.
154. ibid. p. 54.
155. ibid. pp. 54-5.
156. 'Abdu'l-Bahá, *Tablets*, vol. 1, p. iii.
157. Nida, *Theory and Practice of Translation*, p. 15.
158. Rabbaní, *Priceless Pearl*, pp. 196-7.
159. ibid. p. 196.
160. ibid. p. 203.
161. Nida, *Theory and Practice of Translation*, pp. 28-9.

162. Rabbaní, *Priceless Pearl*, p. 197.
163. ibid. pp. 197-8.
164. Toury, *In Search of a Theory of Translation*, p. 43.
165. *The Six Year Plan: 1986-1992*, p. 116.
166. Shoghi Effendi, Foreword to Bahá'u'lláh, *Kitáb-i-Íqán*, p. v.
167. Shoghi Effendi, *God Passes By*, p. 325.
168. 'Abdu'l-Bahá, *Will and Testament*, p. 11.
169. ibid. p. 14.
170. ibid.
171. ibid. p. 15.
172. ibid. p. 12.
173. ibid.
174. ibid.
175. ibid. p. 20.
176. ibid. pp. 11-12.
177. ibid. pp. 25-6.
178. Rabbaní, *Priceless Pearl*, pp. 81-2.
179. ibid. p. 341.
180. ibid. p. 343.
181. Collins, 'A Tribute to Shoghi Effendi', p. 8.
182. Rabbaní, *Priceless Pearl*, p. 393.
183. Rabbaní, *Twenty-Five Years of the Guardianship*, pp. 15-16.